Dynamic Cover Letters

Dynamic Cover Letters

Revised

How to Write the Letter That Gets You the Job

Katharine Hansen and Randall S. Hansen, Ph.D.

Ten Speed Press

Berkeley / Toronto

Ten Speed Press
PO Box 7123
Berkeley, California 94707
www.tenspeed.com

Distributed in Australia by Simon & Schuster Australia; in Canada by Ten Speed Press Canada; in New Zealand by Southern Publishers Group; in South Africa by Real Books; in Singapore and Malaysia by Berkeley Books; and in the United Kingdom and Europe by Airlift Books.

Cover and text design by Paul Kepple @ Headcase Design

Library of Congress Cataloging-in-Publication Data

Hansen, Katharine.
     Dynamic cover letters: how to write the letter that gets you the job/ Katharine Hansen and Randall S. Hansen.—Rev.
     p. cm.
     Includes bibliographical references and index.
     ISBN 1-58008-227-0 (pbk.)
     1. Cover letters. 2. College graduates—Employment. I. Hansen, Randall S. II. Title.

HF5383 .H278 2001
650.14—dc21   2001001007

Printed in Canada

2 3 4 5 6 7 8 9 10 — 05 04 03 02

To Three Special Men

- William Dayton Sumner

- John N. Sumner

- David L. Rhody

The authors wish to thank the wonderful folks at Ten Speed for their years of dedication and faith in all our work, and all the successful job-seekers who have used our books.

For information about all aspects of career development and job-hunting—especially cover letters—please visit the authors' Web site, Quintessential Careers: The Guide to College, Careers, and Jobs. URL: http://www.quintcareers.com/

Contents

Introduction to the Third Edition

So many aspects of job-hunting have changed in the ten-plus years since we wrote the first edition of this book—and we discuss all of the key changes in this edition. Still, one thing about job-hunting remains the same: a dynamic cover letter is a key tool to your successful job search.

Experts on job-hunting say the purpose of a resume is not to get you a job, but to get you an interview. Yet, the only way you will get an interview is if the employer reads your resume. Your cover letter is the first thing a potential employer will see—and the best way to ensure that she'll go on to read your resume is to write a dynamic cover letter that will arouse her interest. This book shows you how to write a dynamic cover letter.

No matter what the current trends are in the job-hunting market, the job-seeker will always need every competitive edge. A well-crafted, attention-getting, assertive cover letter can provide that edge. This new, expanded edition of *Dynamic Cover Letters* shows you even more ways to write a winning letter. We offer seventy-five effective cover-letter samples, for virtually every type of job-hunting situation. We've beefed up the section on editing your letter. Three new cover-letter makeovers show you how to address specific problems in your letter. Our "Cover Letter Hall of Shame" shows you how *not* to write your cover letter. And because now, more than ever, you need to understand the job-hunting process, we've also expanded "The Big Picture" to give you a quick overview of everything you need to know to market yourself, and revised "Job-Hunting on the Internet" to help both the novice and experienced job-seeker. Finally, to make the process a little more fun, after reading all about cover letters you can test your knowledge with the "Cover Letter Quiz."

We wish you much success—in using this book to develop *your* dynamic cover letters, and in your job search.

—Katharine Hansen and Randall S. Hansen, Ph.D.

Send Not Thy Resume Naked into the World

What is a cover letter? It's also known as a letter of introduction, letter of application, transmittal letter, or broadcast letter—and no smart job-seeker should send his or her resume without one. Few employers seriously consider a resume that is not accompanied by a cover letter; thus, a dynamically written cover letter must be part of your job-search strategy.

Why is a cover letter so important? A resume is useless to an employer if he or she doesn't know what kind of work you want to do. A cover letter tells the employer the type of position you're seeking—and exactly how you are qualified for that position.

A dynamic cover letter can give you an edge in the competitive world of job-hunting. The experts say that only two to five of every hundred resumes survive the screening process. Clearly, you can increase your chances of being invited for an interview by writing an effective cover letter.

This point is especially true because few applicants give much thought to their cover letters, even though they have poured blood, sweat, and tears into their resumes. As the applicant who has taken pains to write a striking letter, you will stand out.

The cover letter is particularly useful if you don't have much relevant experience to put into a resume. It takes much less effort to write a cover letter that demonstrates you're the right person for the job—despite your lack of experience—than it does to actually obtain enough experience to beef up a skimpy resume.

A cover letter highlights the aspects of your experience that are most useful to the potential employer, and you can earn points for knowing what those aspects are. Employers get hundreds of resumes, especially when they advertise a choice position. Employers are also very busy. Often the person screening resumes skims each for only a few seconds. Your cover letter can call attention to the skills, talents, and experience the employer is looking for.

Your cover letter provides the opportunity to show what you know about the field you're interested in and the company you're writing to, as well as your written communication skills. Although some employers place a higher premium on writing skills than others, there are few positions in which the ability to write clearly is not an asset. A well-constructed cover letter can also demonstrate your ability to organize your thoughts and get to the point.

Your letter can explain things that your resume can't. If you have large gaps in your employment history or you are reentering the job market or changing the focus of your career, a cover letter can explain these circumstances in a positive way.

A cover letter can serve the same function as the "job objective" on your resume, and expand upon it. Some applicants are reluctant to limit themselves by putting an objective on their resume. Although it is best for a job-seeker to target the type of work desired as specifically as possible, you may be open to more than one option.

Finally, a cover letter is a little window into your personality. A good cover letter can make an employer think, *I'd like to interview this person; she sounds like someone I'd like to get to know better. She seems like just the kind of dynamic person this company needs.*

A cover letter is perhaps the most important part of a direct-mail sales package. The product is you. As with any other sales letter, you are trying to motivate a specific action. You want that employer to call and invite you for an interview. A dynamic cover letter can attract the employer's attention and arouse interest.

So, when should you send a cover letter? Any time you send out your resume. Never send your resume without a cover letter. Even when employers don't specifically ask for a cover letter in their ads or job postings, they expect one. The only exception is when an ad states "resumes only." Employers often make this restriction when they expect a large number of responses and they plan to use some standard screening device. An increasing number of firms, especially in the technology fields, scan all the resumes they receive into a database so that they can program the computer to screen resumes that don't match their specifications. If you make the cut, the employer then may ask you for a cover letter. See page 51 for more information about scanning.

Three Kinds of Cover Letters

There are roughly three kinds of cover letters, each corresponding to a different method of job-hunting. Most successful job-seekers will find that they do not employ any one method or use any one kind of cover letter, but rather a combination of all three. To understand the three kinds of cover letters, it is helpful to look at the three types of job searches you'll use them for.

Only about one-fifth of the job market is what we call "open." That means that only about 20 percent of job openings are ever publicly known. The main avenue for informing the public about these openings is through want ads in the newspaper, trade magazines, and other publications, as well as job-posting ads on various Web sites.

Employment agencies and executive-search firms are another source of these open-market positions. The first kind of cover letter, used to respond to these public notices, is the invited letter.

The other fourth-fifths of the job market is "closed," meaning you can't find out about the positions unless you dig. That digging most often takes the form of compiling a list of all the companies in your field that you might be interested in working for and contacting them to ask for an interview. Obviously, that means some job-seekers will send out a great many resumes—accompanied by the type of cover letter that we call the uninvited or cold-contact letter—sometimes blanketing a given field of companies with direct-mail packages. This job-search tool can be very effective, especially if you have a specific set of companies you wish to work for or are looking to work in a specific geographic location.

The successful job-seeker will persist in following up on the interviews he or she asks for, even when the employer says there are no openings. Will the employer be annoyed with you for persisting in seeking an interview? Probably not—employers admire drive and ambition. Your persistence means you truly want to work for that company. When we were hiring, the "squeaky wheel gets the grease" approach worked on us almost every time. Just make sure you don't overdo it and end up annoying the employer.

A job-hunter who can get a few minutes of an employer's time can succeed in a number of ways. By finding out more about the company's needs, you may be able to create a position for yourself even though the employer has said no openings exist. More likely, however, you will learn a little more about your field—knowledge that you can apply to your job search.

Best of all, you can close the interview by saying, "I'm sorry to hear you have no openings, but perhaps you could suggest someone else in the field who does." If you've made a good impression in your interview, chances are the employer will give you not just one but several referrals.

And that leads us to the third kind of cover letter, a very close cousin to the uninvited letter. This letter, too, is uninvited, but it has an edge. It prominently displays the name of a person your addressee knows. We call this kind of cover letter the referral letter. Referral letters are the product of networking (see page 72), which most experts say is the most effective method of job-hunting.

A referral letter will start out, for example, "John Ross of Technology Unlimited suggested you might have openings for systems analysts."

Referral letters can come about from a variety of sources. You might talk with someone at a meeting of a trade association in your field who will tell you of an opening she knows of. An acquaintance at a party might tell you of someone he knows whose company could use an employee with your experience. A friend might tell you about a job she saw through her company's internal job-posting.

The method of job-hunting you choose will depend a great deal on your situation. If you already have a job and are interested in moving on but not desperate to get a new job, you may be content to read the help-wanted ads in your Sunday newspaper or the job postings on your favorite Web site and respond to those that appeal to you.

If, however, you are mounting a major job search or are a recent graduate, you will probably conduct a more aggressive mass-mailing campaign, as well as monitoring the job ads closely and networking to seek contacts who can refer you to where the openings might be.

Next, we'll look at some of the characteristics peculiar to each kind of cover letter.

The Uninvited or Cold-Contact Cover Letter

The uninvited letter is the most straightforward and has several advantages. Most importantly, it enables you to address the letter to the person who has the power to give you a job, if you can manage to find out who that is. This point is key. Whenever possible, any cover letter should be sent to a named individual; with the uninvited letter this advice is especially important. The largest employer in Central Florida, for instance, throws away any letter that does not address him by name. If you want to get an interview and hence a job, you can forget about using such salutations as "Dear Sir or Madam," "Gentlemen," "Dear Human Resources Director," or "To Whom It May Concern." Those salutations tell the employer that you were not concerned enough to find out whom it concerns. We'll talk later about how to find out the names of the best person to address.

The uninvited cover letter provides an opportunity to show what you know about the company you're writing to. Demonstrating that you've done your homework is a good way to get a real edge on your competition. How many times, after all, have you been asked during an interview, "What do you know about our company?" Many employers use your knowledge of the company as a litmus test.

The uninvited cover letter enables you to take a proactive approach to job-hunting instead of the reactive approach, in which you merely answer ads. It can be a great tool for uncovering hidden jobs where supposedly no openings exist. Your letter can make such an impression that you'll be remembered as soon as a vacancy opens up. You may also be able to create an opening for yourself by convincing the employer that the company needs someone with your talents. At the very least, you may obtain an interview in which the employer can refer you to others in the field who might have use for you.

The biggest disadvantage of the uninvited cover letter is that it is, after all, uninvited. When an employer doesn't have a current opening and hasn't solicited your letter and resume, he or she is likely to give it much less attention than if an opening had been advertised. You can minimize this disadvantage by writing a letter that lets the employer know that you are someone he or she should pay attention to.

A key aspect of a successful direct-mail campaign with this letter is compiling a large list of potential employers—perhaps as many as several hundred. You must also research each company, to individualize your letters. We won't deal too extensively here with list compilation and research since our main focus is cover letters. A number of good books, however, offer general job-hunting techniques and deal extensively with developing job leads and researching potential employers. Several of these books are cited in "Recommended Reading," page 163. You'll also find a list of sources for hidden job opportunities on page 73. We've also included an extensive list of "Key Career and Job Web Sites," page 160.

The Invited Cover Letter

A cover letter that is invited through a job ad offers the primary advantage that the employer expects and welcomes it; he or she has an opening, may be very anxious to fill it, and is hoping you will be the right person.

The invited cover letter also enables you to speak to the requirements of the ad. You can offer the employer the requirements sought because you *know* the requirements sought; it's all spelled out in the ad.

Whether or not you can write to a specific individual and demonstrate your knowledge of the company the same way you can with the uninvited letter depends on which of two types of job ad you are responding to.

Many ads reveal the name of the company that placed the ad. When you know what company you're responding to, you can use the same strategies as with the uninvited letter: You can research the company and demonstrate your knowledge in your letter, and also find out the best person to write to—unless the ad already specifies the person the company wants you to write to.

Sometimes companies, for various reasons, place blind ads, which do not identify the company seeking the employee. Companies place these ads because they don't want their current employees to know they are trying to fill a position, or because they expect a large response and don't want the obligation of responding to every applicant.

Some blind ads are more blind than others. Some use initials for the company name; others, only an address or post office box. In those cases, it may still be possible to find out which company is advertising. If you can do so, you can demonstrate your knowledge of the company, and the employer will most likely be impressed with your resourcefulness in identifying the firm.

In her book *Put Your Degree to Work,* Marcia Fox tells a story about an ad that referred applicants to a "J. M. Smith." Only 1 of 300 respondents bothered to call the company and ask the full name of "J. M. Smith." Janet M. Smith appreciated the single letter addressed to her and was impressed with the motivation of the job-seeker who had made the effort to learn her name. That job-seeker was also one of only three people interviewed for the position. Imagine the poor job-seekers who addressed their letters to "Mr. Smith"; an example of the importance of avoiding the use of sexist salutations.

This same concept applies to situations when the ad asks you to write to "Human Resources Director." If you know the name of the company, instead of addressing the letter to the Human Resources Director, find out the name of the human resources director, and address the letter to him.

The blindest of blind ads gives only a box number at the newspaper carrying the advertisement. The employer rents a box at the newspaper and uses it as an address to which applicants should respond. There is virtually no way to find out which company is advertising. Thus, you can't address your letter to a named individual, and you can't talk about your knowledge of the company.

To whom should you address your letter when you don't know who the advertiser is? As mentioned earlier, avoid "To Whom It May Concern." "Gentlemen" is sexist. "Dear Sir or Madam" is acceptable, if a bit stilted and old-fashioned. We have often used "Dear Friends" as a cordial, nonsexist salutation, although some career experts have said it is too informal. Another favorite of ours for blind-box ads is "Dear Boxholder." Finally, you could use "Dear Hiring Manager for [name of position]."

It is also acceptable when responding to a blind-box ad to omit the salutation and begin with the body of the letter.

The Referral Letter

The value of the referral letter is in its name-dropping. If you can grab the potential employer's attention by mentioning someone he knows and respects in the first line of the letter, you will have gained a terrific advantage over the competition. Some variations on the referral letter include approaches like these:

- "I met with Mary Jones last week, and she mentioned that you might have a need for someone with a background in book marketing."
- "My adviser, Claude Brachfeld, never misses an opportunity to tell me of your innovations in the superconductivity field."

It would be a rare employer who would fail to interview an applicant with such an edge. How do you find the people to use in referral letters? Through networking, a key job-hunting tool. In its simplest form, networking involves using everyone you know as a resource to finding a new job. You can find much more about networking in the networking section of this book, page 72, and in one of our other publications, *A Foot in the Door* (Ten Speed, 2000). Online networking resources can be found in "Key Career and Job Web Sites," page 160.

There is also such a thing as a self-referred cover letter, which results when you call the employer before sending a cover letter and resume. Sometimes employers will put only their phone number in an ad even though they are really looking for letters and resumes, so they can do some preliminary screening by phone. They'll ask only those who sound qualified to send their resumes. So, you call up, and the employer asks you to send her your resume. When you write to her, you remind her of the conversation: "I enjoyed chatting with you this morning about the opening in your art department. As you recall, I told you I have the experience with desktop publishing that you're looking for . . ."

There are other occasions when you may find it useful to call the employer and follow up with a self-referred letter. For instance, you might call at the suggestion of a friend who works at the company and says there are openings you would be right for. Self-referrals can also spring from summer jobs, internships, informational interviews, meeting an employer at a career fair, or a social encounter.

The Basics

If you don't know where to begin with writing a cover letter, you can follow a formula. We stress *can* because the most important advice we can give you about this formula and the many sample cover letters at the back of this book is: Don't be afraid to deviate from the formula. Keep in mind the type of job you are applying for (because creative jobs allow you to be more creative in your cover letters) and the culture of the company and industry (because some companies, such as those in the Internet field, also allow you more creativity). Feel free to steal phrases, words, and basic structures to your heart's content, but adapt each cover letter to the specific situation. Be a professional and write your own letters.

It's critical that your letter is unique and specific to you—not one that any applicant could have written. Employers can smell a formula a mile away, yet most job-hunters insist on writing letters that sound the same as every other cover letter. As a result, most cover letters are insufferably dull. You'll make the employer's day if you write an interesting letter. We've had employers call us just to compliment us on our cover letters even when, for one reason or another, they weren't able to hire us.

If you're having trouble getting started, see the worksheets on pages 21 and 22.

The Cover Letter Formula

First paragraph: Tell why you're writing, in such a way as to arouse the employer's interest. Use this paragraph to display your specific knowledge about the company you're writing to. You *must* grab the employer's attention. Avoid openings such as "I'm writing to you in response to your ad for a nutritionist in the Sunday *Los Angeles Times*." See "Attention-Grabbing Beginnings." Identify the job title or general area you're interested in. The reader shouldn't have to guess what kind of job you're looking for.

Second paragraph: Briefly describe your professional and/or academic qualifications. Cite examples of your qualifications for the position sought. Draw on the power of your resume and refer to it—better yet, expand on it. Avoid trite, overused phrases, such as "as you will note in my enclosed resume" or "I have taken the liberty of enclosing my resume." If you are short on job experience, mention extracurricular activities, especially examples of leadership, special projects you worked on, or the fact that you worked your way through school. If you're a homemaker returning to the workforce, don't forget to include volunteer work and family-management skills.

Third paragraph: Relate yourself to the company. Provide details as to why you should be considered. Use this paragraph to show off your research on the company and the industry. If you can't research the company, then use this paragraph to expand on your qualifications.

Fourth paragraph: Request action. Ask for an interview appointment. Suggest dates on which you're available. Tell the employer that you will call to make an appointment. *Be sure to follow up!* It's a lot harder for the employer to ignore a request for action than a wishy-washy "call me if you're interested" approach.

Before closing: Thank the prospective employer for his or her time and consideration.

Dear So and So

The best way to find out who should receive your letter is to call the company and ask the receptionist. For example, "Could you tell me who does the hiring for financial analyst positions?" If you've been employed before, you know what we're talking about. Receptionists and key administrative assistants—the company's "gatekeepers"—know everyone and everything that is going on in the company, and they can be a key resource for you in obtaining the name of the hiring manager.

If the receptionist refers you to the human resources department, ask also for the name of the company president. If you must choose between sending your letter to a human resources director and the company president, send it to the president (unless it's a very large company, in which case you should ask for the head of the department in which you're interested in working).

Yes, it's true, the president may never see that mail. A secretary or other lower-echelon staffer will probably open and screen the president's mail, but whoever handles it is responsible for responding to the president's mail and making certain the president's image isn't damaged by failing to respond to a correspondent. The underling has to report back to the president on what action was taken; thus, a chain of communication is initiated centering around your letter.

Chances are your letter will end up back in the human resources office anyway, but if you send it to the president you will increase the chances of someone with real hiring power seeing it along the way.

Attention-Grabbing Beginnings

The biggest trick to composing a dynamic cover letter is to begin it in a way that will draw the reader in and make him or her want to read more—and ultimately read your resume and invite you for an interview. And you may have as little as twenty seconds to grab that person's attention.

Let's look at it this way: A 1999 study funded by Pitney-Bowes revealed that the average worker receives 190 messages a day of all kinds—faxes, emails, phone calls, letters, memos, air-express deliveries, people just stopping by to chat. Most workers have to actually stop their work to deal with messages at least three times an hour, and 40 percent are interrupted six or more times an hour. These results show that the busy hiring manager has very little time to spend on each piece of communication crossing his or her desk, so your letter needs to get attention in a hurry to be effective.

Some ways to grab the employer's attention include demonstrating your accomplishments, beginning with a quote, starting with a clever angle, praising the employer you're writing to, and even pasting a copy of the job ad to your letter. Remember, though, that the key to a successful letter is an introductory paragraph that makes the reader want to read more.

Demonstrating Your Accomplishments

Perhaps the simplest and most straightforward method of grabbing a potential employer's attention is by telling her the two or three key accomplishments, skills, or experiences you possess that make you the ideal candidate for the job and will make her job easier.

Quotes

Using a meaningful quote from someone in your field can be an attention-getting way to start your letter. You should be sure that the quote is truly meaningful to the job you're seeking, and was spoken by someone your reader is likely to respect. Make sure also that your quote isn't too long. No matter how good it is, if it's too long your reader is bound to wonder when you're going to get to the point, and may stop reading halfway through.

The Clever Angle

Once in a while, you may be able to come up with an approach that is out of the ordinary and shows your creativity (see the samples starting on page 122). If you're applying for a job in a creative field such as journalism, advertising, art, or even sales—or applying for a job in an industry known for its informality or creativity, such as Internet companies—you can take more risks than if you're applying as an engineer, for instance. Again, be sure that what you're saying applies to the situation and isn't too long.

Praising the Employer

What employer wouldn't warm up to an applicant who talks about how much he admires the company he's applying to and how much he'd like to work there—and why? Praise for the employer is often a good approach, but you can make it infinitely more credible by supporting your praise with facts that show how much you know about the firm.

Pasting a Copy of the Ad to Your Letter

When responding to a want ad, you can direct your reader's attention to your reason for writing by pasting a copy of the ad right on the letter. This technique is particularly effective when writing to a large company that regularly advertises openings, as the recipient can tell immediately which ad you're responding to. Seeing the ad will also refresh his or her memory about what the ad is asking for—and if you've tailored your letter well to the requirements of the ad, your reader just may end up with the impression that you're the perfect person for the job. Obviously, this approach is not a good idea if your qualifications don't quite match the requirements of the ad.

The Body of the Letter

Once you've tackled identifying the person you are writing to and decided how your letter can grab attention, the next step is developing the content for the letter's body. In this chapter, we discuss some key issues you need to think about when developing the content for the remainder of your letter.

Your Unique Selling Proposition

There's an advertising term that you should think about when you are composing the body of your letter: the Unique Selling Proposition. When companies are trying to determine how to market a product, they focus on the Unique Selling Proposition (USP). It's the one thing that makes that product different from any other. The USP may be a lower price, more convenient packaging, a better taste or smell. Whatever it may be, the company thinks this USP will make consumers prefer the product to others just like it.

When preparing to write a cover letter, you may find it helpful to think about your own USP. What is the one thing that makes you unique—and better than any other candidate applying for a similar position with this company? What can you offer that no other applicant can? What is the one reason the employer should want to hire you above all other candidates? If you can determine your USP and build it into a dynamic paragraph, you will have a real advantage in creating a dynamic cover letter.

Broadcasting Your Accomplishments .

To gather plenty of material for the body of your cover letters, make lists of your accomplishments in each of your past positions or in your academic career. Try to list at least three major accomplishments from each position. Think of ways in which you left each company or department better than you found it. From that list, choose about three accomplishments that are most relevant to the position you're applying for.

The Screening Process .

When answering job ads, you should speak to the requirements of the ad. Even if your experience does not exactly match what is being asked for in the ad, you can sometimes still make a case for yourself in your cover letter. However, the first person who reads your letter may not have the power and wisdom to decide that you are a worthwhile candidate despite the lack of a perfect match. That person may be a clerk or other subordinate, screening letters according to whether or not the qualifications match the exact requirements stated in the ad. Therefore, it's important to make the match seem as close as possible. And if your letter is being scanned into a database (see "Scanning," page 51), using the right keywords becomes even more important. Pick out key phrases and adapt them to your experience.

If the person screening the letter is looking for someone with, say, two to three years of experience, it may actually hurt you if you have considerably more experience, because the numbers won't match up. Say that you have "more than two to three years experience," and the screener will see the magic "two to three."

Turning a No into a Yes .

Imagine an ad that says, "Must have experience placing press releases in publications." Let's say you don't have that particular experience, but all your other qualifications match the requirements of the ad. You might decide to write something like this: "Although I don't have experience placing press releases in publications, my experience as an editor has shown me what editors are looking for in the releases they publish." This is a step in the right direction, but a bit too negative.

To develop a more positive, sales-oriented way of addressing the lack of experience in your cover letter, picture an employer asking the same question in an interview: "Do you

12

have experience placing press releases in publications?" If you respond, "No, but my experience as an editor . . ." you automatically have a strike against you because the employer doesn't want to hear "no."

The same thing applies in your cover letter. Don't say: "Although I don't have experience placing press releases in publications . . ." Instead, simply use the rest of the sentence: "My experience as an editor has shown me what editors are looking for in the press releases they publish."

You've turned a "no" into a "yes" and made it look as though you meet the requirements of the ad when you don't quite. Yet, you were completely honest. See Stacey Greene's letter on page 26 for an example of how an applicant turns a "no" into a "yes."

Transferable Skills .

What if you're a recent college grad without much job experience—or a job-seeker looking to make a career change? You should exploit transferable skills. What are transferable skills? Simply put, they are skills you have acquired during any activity in your life—jobs, classes, projects, parenting, hobbies, sports—virtually anything that is transferable and applicable to what you want to do in your next job. Think of everything you've done in terms of how it is transferable to what you want to be doing—and portray it that way. (You can read more about using transferable skills on this page of our Quintessential Careers Web site: http://www.quintcareers.com/transferable_skills.html.)

The Bottom Line .

The job-seeker should always remember that most businesses are there to make money. Employers would like to know that you can help them make money or at least help them not spend so much. Never lose an opportunity to tell the employer how you can make money for the company, improve sales, reduce costs, or cut waste. An easy way to remember this concept is the PEP formula: Profitability, Efficiency, Productivity.

Two Magic Words .

Two words we try not to leave out of any cover letter are "contribution" and "success." We almost always use "contribution" in the first paragraph: "My solid editing experience would enable me to make a meaningful contribution to the managing editor position you are currently advertising." This practice follows the philosophy of telling the employer what you can do for him or her—how you can help his or her bottom line. Employers appreciate the attitude that you want to contribute to the company.

And, nothing succeeds like success. We always make a point of telling the employer how we succeeded in at least one area of our experience. "Success" is a confident word. Employers like an applicant who considers himself or herself a success.

Tips for a Dynamic Format

Employers scan cover letters quickly. Thus, anything you can do to make your special qualifications stand out will give you an edge. Three ways to accent your special qualities are highlighting, quantifying, and demonstrating your ideas.

Highlighting

Some good examples of highlighting can be found on pages 117 through 121 in the sample letters section. These job-seekers have used formats that make their accomplishments stand out—and make it easier for the reader to note them at a glance. Highlighting is also a great technique to use when you are tailoring your letter to the requirements of an ad (the sample letter on page 119 is a nice example). One way to do it is by listing special accomplishments and setting them off with numbers or bullets (those little marks that accent items on a list such as ❏, ●, or ✓). In a word-processing program, you can use the automated numbered-list or bulleted-list feature. You can also set off your list by indenting it. You can highlight words, phrases, and accomplishments by underlining them or making them bold.

Quantifying

Numbers talk. Sometimes numbers are the best way to drive home a point about your achievements. State how many people you supervised, how many customers you handled, how much money you saved the company, by what percentage sales increased in your department during your tenure. You can also say things like:

- "I was circulation director for a newspaper with a circulation of 100,000."
- "My experience includes creative supervision at the largest ad agency in Tucson."
- "I supervised telephone installation requests in the second-largest city in Massachusetts."

Demonstrating Your Ideas .

An employer can hardly help being impressed by an applicant who has learned so much about the field and/or the company that he can offer his ideas for boosting the company's profitability or efficiency. The best setting for an employer to hear your ideas is in the interview, but to make sure you get the interview, you might want to whet the employer's appetite by revealing a couple of ideas in your cover letter. Remember not to give away too much for free. Just tease the employer with your ingenuity enough so she'll want to hear more.

Closing Your Letter .

After thanking the employer for her time and for considering you for a position, you can sign off with a standard business-letter closing: "Sincerely," "Best regards," or "Cordially."

Don't forget to sign your letter. And do sign boldly and confidently—some experts suggest that a felt-tip pen will produce an appropriately bold, confident signature. Blue ink is preferred because it assures the employer that your letter is not a photocopy.

Adding a Postscript .

Some job-hunting experts, such as Brian Krueger (author of *College Grad Job Hunter*), suggest that adding a postscript—especially one that's handwritten—will make your letter stand out. The postscript should restate your Unique Selling Proposition in a new way. "I guarantee it will be the first thing read on your cover letter," Krueger writes. Here are some sample USPs that could be used as postscripts:

- *P.S. My solid marketing background and creative flair will enable me to help you create new products that will fly off the shelves.*

• *P.S. With my proven track record of revamping inventory systems, I am just the person you need as director of inventory control systems.*

Avoiding the Three Most Common Mistakes

After reviewing thousands of cover letters and talking to countless employers, we can promise you that your cover letter will stand out from the crowd—and avoid the employer's trash can or recycling bin—if you avoid these three very common cover letter mistakes:

(1) **Not addressing your letter to a named individual.** The *only* time it is acceptable not to address your letter to a person is when you have no way to find out the name of the person with the hiring power for that particular job—such as with a blind-box classified ad or when a job posting lists the title of the hiring manager, but doesn't list the company. In all other cases, you need to make the extra effort to track down the name of the individual with the hiring power and address your letter to that person.

(2) **Failing to request an interview.** As we've already noted, you need to close the sale by asking for an interview. Don't leave the ball in the employer's court. We're all taught to be humble, but now is not the time. You will be far more likely to get an interview if you:

• take the initiative in your letter to ask for the interview,

• tell the employer in the letter that you will follow up, and

• actually do follow up.

(3) **Telling what the company can do for you rather than what you can do for the company.** We've seen too many letters that say something like, "It's been a lifelong dream for me to work at Coca-Cola," or "Working for Amazon.com would be the highlight of my career thus far." Employers want workers who can solve problems, make money for the company, and be productive. Fulfilling your lifelong dream is fairly far down on the list of the employer's priorities. You should always focus on telling the employer how you can contribute to the organization's success.

Do's and Don'ts

Don't ever send your resume without a cover letter.

Do address your letter to a named individual.

Don't use a sexist salutation, such as "Gentlemen," when answering a blind ad.

Don't be negative or too humble.

Do project confidence. For some fields, such as sales or a creative field, it may be okay for your confidence to border on cockiness. Just **Don't** be arrogant.

Don't use such clichés as "Enclosed please find my resume" or "As you can see on my resume enclosed herewith." Employers can see that your resume is enclosed; they don't need you to tell them. Such trite phrases just waste precious space.

Don't leave the ball in the employer's court. Don't say things like, "If you are interested in someone with my qualifications, please feel free to call me to arrange an interview" or "I look forward to hearing from you." **Don't** depend on the employer to take action. Request action. Request an interview, and tell the employer when you will follow up to arrange it. Then, **Do So.** It is imperative that you follow up. You will greatly increase your chances of getting interviews if you call the employer after writing instead of sitting back and waiting for a call. Those who wait for the employer to call them will generally have a long wait indeed.

Do make the most of your opening paragraph by using an attention-grabbing beginning.

Don't send a cover letter that contains any typos, misspellings, incorrect grammar or punctuation, smudges, or grease from yesterday's lunch.

Do use simple language and uncomplicated sentence structure. Ruthlessly eliminate all unnecessary words. Follow the journalist's credo: Write tight!

Do speak to the requirements of the job, especially when responding to an ad.

Don't send letters that are obviously photocopied or otherwise mass-produced.

Do send an original letter to each employer.

Don't include a salary requirement unless the employer requests it; even then, including any information about salary may be risky (see "Sticky Issues," page 56).

Do imagine yourself in the prospective employer's position. What would you look for in a cover letter? What would turn you off? What would you consider vital information and what would you rather not see?

Do keep it brief. **Never, Never** more than one page, and it's best to keep it well under a full page. Each paragraph should have no more than one to three sentences. You may think there is important information that you can't possibly leave out, but rest assured, a busy employer will never read it all. The longer your letter appears, the more daunting it is. If it looks hopelessly long, it may never be read at all.

Don't write your letter by hand unless the ad requests it.

Don't tell the employer what he or she can do for you.

Do tell the employer how you can meet his or her needs and contribute to the company. To paraphrase John F. Kennedy, ask not what the company can do for you, tell what you can do for the company.

If you're a recent graduate, **Don't** forget that the employer's frame of reference is different from a professor's or admissions officer's. He or she may think it's nice that your grade-point average is high or that you got an A in a particularly tough course, but that grade rarely means much in a professional context. An employer will be more impressed that you worked your way through school and/or took advantage of every internship opportunity.

Don't be overly solicitous or plead for favors. Your qualifications should stand on their own.

Do try to answer the question that the employer will be asking while reading your letter: "Why should I hire this person?" Answer with your Unique Selling Proposition.

Don't rehash your resume. You can use your cover letter to highlight the aspects of your resume that are relevant to the position, but you're wasting precious space—and the potential employer's time—if you simply repeat your resume.

Don't try to include too much detail or be too general. Hone in on the pithy, precise descriptions of the accomplishments that qualify you for the job.

Don't make the employer dig through the letter to discover what kind of job you're seeking.

Don't use vague and nebulous phrases that describe your personal objectives: "I am seeking a responsible, people-oriented position with growth potential." Such a description could apply to hundreds of jobs. It's your responsibility to discover which jobs fulfill those requirements.

Don't list hobbies or personal interests in your letter unless they are somehow relevant to the position, or you happen to know the person you're writing to is passionate about the same interests. We once knew someone who went through a long series of interviews for a marketing position at a golfing magazine. Just when he was sure he had the job, the magazine rejected him. The reason? He didn't play golf. Nothing he could have said in his cover letter would have gotten him the job, but if he had been a golfer and said so in his cover letter, he would have had a clear advantage.

Do be sure the potential employer can reach you. Whenever you know the name of the employer you're writing to, you should follow up and make an interview appointment. However, you should always make sure the employer knows how to reach you in case she wants to call you for an interview before you've had a chance to follow up. If you're writing in response to a blind-box ad, you should, of course, be sure the boxholder knows how to reach you. Your letter should include a phone number that the employer can use to reach you during daytime business hours. It can be your work number if you are able to discreetly receive phone calls at your place of employment. It can be your home number if someone is there during the day to answer the phone or if you have an answering machine or voicemail. Just be sure that whatever number you use is not one that will result in an unanswered phone every time the employer tries to call during business hours. Of course, you can also include your cell phone number and email address, if you have them.

Do job hunt year-round. While company activities slow down during certain times of the year (summers, holidays), job-hunting is no longer a seasonal activity. Take advantage of events such as holiday parties to network.

Do use action verbs. See the list below (and categorized by skill type on the Action Verbs page of our Quintessential Careers Web site: http://www.quintcareers.com/action.html).

Action Verbs

accelerated	doubled	organized	sold
accomplished	edited	performed	solved
achieved	eliminated	planned	sorted
administered	enlarged	prepared	specialized
analyzed	established	presented	stabilized
approved	examined	processed	started
arranged	expanded	programmed	streamlined
bought	facilitated	promoted	strengthened
built	governed	proposed	structured
cataloged	grouped	purchased	succeeded
classified	guided	recommended	summarized
completed	hired	recruited	supervised
conceived	implemented	rectified	systematized
conducted	improved	redesigned	trained
consolidated	increased	reduced	transacted
contracted	indexed	regulated	translated
controlled	interviewed	reorganized	trimmed
coordinated	introduced	represented	tripled
created	invented	researched	turned around
decreased	investigated	reshaped	uncovered
delivered	launched	restructured	unified
demonstrated	maintained	revised	unraveled
designed	managed	saved	widened
developed	moderated	scheduled	won
devised	monitored	serviced	wrote
directed	negotiated	simplified	
distributed	orchestrated		

A Cover-Letter Worksheet

The hardest part of writing a cover letter is getting started. If you're having trouble, a worksheet like the one below may get you going. The example shows how one job-seeker filled out the worksheet, and the following page shows the letter that resulted. On page 22 is a blank, which you may want to photocopy and use to get started on your own letters.

Remember that the worksheet merely provides the skeleton. Once you have the bare bones, you need to develop the letter.

Cover-Letter Worksheet

I am a recent graduate of *Wesleyan College with a Bachelor of Arts in hotel management*

I want a job as *a hotel/motel management trainee*

Here's what I can do for your company (my Unique Selling Proposition):

Summer internship with Hyatt Hotels, getting "real world" experience.

Two years work all phases of hospitality at college-run hotel

Developed cost-efficient check in/check out system that cuts waste

3.8/4.0 GPA while holding down two jobs to pay for education

Hard-working, conscientious, reliable

Winner of Outstanding Graduate Award, Hilton School of Hotel Management

I will contact you *next week* to set up an interview.

Thank you for your time and consideration.

June 14, 2000

Mr. Roger G. Harlon
Starwood Hotels & Resorts
777 Westchester Ave.
White Plains, NY 10604

Dear Mr. Harlon,

I'd like to contribute my sharp hotel-management skills, gained through years of experience, and my bachelor of arts degree in hospitality management, as a management trainee with your hotel chain.

I'm a recent graduate of Wesleyan College—with a grade-point average of 3.8 out of 4.0—and have several years of relevant experience, including:

- Two years in varying levels learning all phases of hospitality management at a college-managed hotel
- Summer internship with Hyatt Hotels

I have put this experience to good use, developing a cost-efficient check-in/check-out system that cut down on waste and saved the college-run hotel an average of $5 per guest. My proven innovation and leadership won me the Outstanding Graduate Award.

I am hard-working, conscientious, and reliable, and I want to put my knowledge and experience to work for your hotel chain.

I will contact you next week to set up an interview.

Thank you for your time and consideration.

Sincerely,

John Donovan

I am a _____

I want a job as _____

Here's what I can do for your company (my Unique Selling Proposition):

_____

_____

_____

_____

_____

_____

I will contact you _____ to set up an interview.

Thank you for your time and consideration.

Editing

After you've composed your cover letter, you should take a red pencil to it and edit mercilessly. Eliminate every unnecessary word. The more concise you can make your letter, the clearer your message will be: short, sweet, and to the point. The more you can say in the least number of words, the more likely the employer is to read and pay attention to your letter.

On the next several pages are a too-long cover letter and its edited, concise version. The job-seeker who wrote it tried to crowd his letter with too much unnecessary detail.

Mr. Salvador was justifiably proud of his academic career. As he indicates in his last paragraph, he believes his background could be useful at a newspaper. But his letter has done nothing to convince the prospective employer of any connection between his academic achievements and what he could do for a newspaper. He may well have a vision of how his academic background would relate to being a municipal reporter or sportswriter, but he has done nothing in his letter to relate his college background to the job. Instead, he has told his entire academic history, although little of it has any relevance to the job he seeks.

His other problem is that his sentences are too long and wordy. The original letter was so long that it went to two pages, a definite no-no in cover letters. Note that, even squeezed onto one page, it is far too wordy and beside-the-point. He needed to remember that his frame of reference, the academic world, is probably very different from the employer's. What sounds impressive in academia may elicit no more than a yawn from any employer seeking an experienced candidate.

While we've edited Mr. Salvador's letter primarily for length and complexity, we provide on the pages following Salvador's letter three cover letter makeovers that target additional challenges common to cover letters:

- presenting yourself as qualified for a job for which you might not seem quite qualified
- writing a cover letter that helps you switch careers
- avoiding writing your autobiography in your cover letter

A must-have source on concise writing and correct word usage is the classic *The Elements of Style* by William Strunk and E. B. White. Macmillan puts out an inexpensive paperback edition. Get it.

To demonstrate some of the more common writing-style problems in cover letters, we've concluded this editing section with a writing-style checklist and editing exercises to help you practice your editing skills.

After you've cut your letter down to size and proofed it carefully for typos, spelling, grammar, syntax, punctuation, and capitalization, put it down for a few hours (if your time frame allows). Come back later and read it as though you were the employer. Does it grab you? Is it compelling? Would it make you want to call the applicant in for an interview?

You can also ask a friend to read your cover letter—ideally someone who has experience screening and hiring, or someone in your field.

Well-known ad executive Jane Trahey had a unique method for discovering her letters' impact. She would write her letter, stick it in an envelope, and mail it to herself. By the time it arrived, she would have virtually forgotten sending it and could approach it with the same degree of subjectivity as a prospective employer. You may want to try this as a test before you need to send a great letter quickly in response to an ad for your dream job. An even faster approach is to email yourself the cover letter—and wait until the next day to read and review it.

Cover Letter Makeovers

Sometimes merely editing for wordiness is not enough. Occasionally a cover letter requires a complete overhaul. The three letters that follow each represent a specific problem that the job-seeker tries to address—with marginal success. We critiqued the letters and then rewrote each in a way that better targets the job-seeker's situation.

December 11, 2000

Mrs. Karen Harper
Editor, Wonderful Publications
P.O. Box 185
Secaucus, NJ 07094

Dear Mrs. Harper,

I am interested in applying for the entry-level Municipal Reporting and Sportswriter positions advertised in the August 20, 2000, edition of the *Nutville Post*. In May of 2000, I graduated from Drew University in Madison, New Jersey with a master of arts degree in political science. In May of 1998, I graduated from Rutgers University with dual bachelor of arts degrees in political science and history. Since my May graduation, I have furthered my studies by completing several courses at Montclair State College.

Enclosed is my resume, which will give you an idea of my interests and achievements in the public affairs and communications areas. Please note that while attending Drew University, I was selected to participate in the Semester on the United Nations program. Twice weekly, I studied at the United Nations and the Drew facilities on United Nations Plaza in a program that included briefings and addresses by members of the Secretariat, the delegations, the specialized agencies, and the nongovernmental organizations represented at the United Nations. Furthermore, please note that while attending Rutgers University, I was selected to join the Iota-Alpha Chapter of Phi Alpha Theta, the International Council of Conspicuous Attainments and Scholarship in the Field of History.

In addition, please note that in selecting my curricula, I emphasized creative writing and development of oral communications skills. As a result, I am able to structure a problem into question form, provide a thesis answer, and support my thesis through qualitative and quantitative methods. Moreover, my three years on the Rutgers University Student Governing Association, two years as president and treasurer of the Rutgers University Political Science Club, and graduate training on team projects at Drew University have given me the ability to address large groups with enthusiasm and clarity.

Similarly, please note that while attending St. Bonaventure High School in Newark, I was selected to serve a three-year term as boys' basketball scorekeeper/statistician and sports-information director. As a consequence, a portion of my responsibilities included the preparation and dissemination of sports information to *The Newark Star-Ledger* and the *Jersey Journal*.

Without hesitation, please contact the following three gentlemen for references: Dr. Walter Miller 201-555-3000. Dr. Kenneth Copwell 201-555-5105. Dr. David Wicker 201-555-6485.

Since I believe my background could be utilized very efficiently by your newspaper, I hope to hear from you regarding a personal interview.

Cordially,

Peter Salvador

December 11, 2000

Mrs. Karen Harper
Editor, Wonderful Publications
P.O. Box 185
Secaucus, NJ 07094

Dear Mrs. Harper,

My strong academic background in political science and government would enable me to make a significant contribution to the municipal reporting position you are currently advertising.

Municipal reporting requires the ability to translate complex governmental issues into simple language for the layperson. My academic career has made me well-versed in government issues. My ability to study and communicate about public affairs was recognized when I was chosen to participate in a special United Nations study program, and selected for membership in a history honor society.

My courses also emphasized creative writing and development of oral communications skills, which would enable me to ask politicians the right questions and communicate the issues clearly to readers.

My leadership abilities and skill in working as a team player may be of eventual interest to you as you promote reporters to editing positions. I have been involved in student government, held office in a political-science club, and worked on team projects during my graduate training.

I am also interested in the sports writing position you advertised, and my three years as a school team statistician and sports-information director show I am equally capable of communicating about sports. I demonstrated my ability to assemble sports material for publication by preparing team reports for the *Newark Star-Ledger* and the *Jersey Journal*.

I'll give you a call next week to arrange a personal interview.

Cordially,

Peter Salvador

November 6, 2000

Mr. Edward Rivera
State Farm Insurance Cos.
1 State Farm Plaza
Bloomington, IL 61710

Dear Mr. Rivera:

I would like to apply for the marketing-research manager position that you advertised in the Chicago Tribune. I believe I could be an asset to your firm as I am very interested in such a research management position. My current position is market research and sales support. I would like to stay on the research side and move more toward management.

I feel that I am qualified and could grow into the position although I have not been employed as a research manager. However I can bring a more diverse background and a strong desire to learn. Outside of my current job I have been involved in various aspects of research projects. I have conducted survey research for a professional organization based in Chicago by utilizing the Internet as a population base. I have conducted various consulting projects for nonprofit organizations in my community. Finally, I have been involved in numerous focus groups, both as a participant and as a moderator.

While I have no direct management experience, I do believe that my background of working with people, both individually and in committees, provides me with the insight needed to be a successful manager.

Please consider me for this position as I think I could contribute a great deal. Feel free to contact me so we can get together and discuss this further.

Sincerely,

Stacey Greene
Research Analyst
Spiegel, Inc.

The Problem

Stacey Green is answering an ad for a job for which she doesn't quite feel qualified. Her challenge is to be honest about her qualifications yet not sound too negative about her weaknesses. In other words, she wishes to turn a "no" into a "yes." What she must remember above all is that the mission of the cover letter is to help secure an interview. She doesn't have to reveal at this point every aspect of her career; she can save that for the interview. Yet, she also doesn't want to misrepresent herself.

Greene also uses several of the phrases that we strongly urge all cover letter writers to avoid: "I feel," "I believe," "I think." Using these phrases dilutes the strength of your assertion. Compare the weakness of "I feel I am qualified" with the strength of "I am qualified." Or the tentativeness of "I think I could contribute" with the conviction of "I am confident that I could contribute."

Body of Greene's Letter, Critiqued

I would like to apply for the marketing-research manager position that you advertised in the Chicago Tribune. I believe I could be an asset to your firm as I am very interested in such a research management position. My current position is market research and sales support. I would like to stay on the research side and move more toward management.

Not a bad opening, but it could be tightened and restructured for greater impact. She also needs to avoid using "I believe." Finally, being "very interested" is no indicator of being an asset in the position.

I feel that I am qualified and could grow into the position although I have not been employed as a research manager. However I can bring a more diverse background and a strong desire to learn.

It's always a tricky situation when you're applying for a job that is a bit of a stretch. You want to be honest, but you don't want to sound too negative. Here, Greene does sound a bit too negative. She can make this point sound more positive without being dishonest, and she needs to be more confident by eliminating the "I feel."

She should definitely skip the phrase "a strong desire to learn." Most companies are far more concerned with profitability, efficiency, and productivity than with teaching their employees. They don't want to be reminded of the time and money investment they have to make in new employees. Given a choice between a candidate who was fully qualified and one with "a strong desire to learn," which one do you think the employer will choose? Greene needs to make herself sound fully qualified without being dishonest. Tricky, indeed.

Outside of my current job I have been involved in various aspects of research projects. I have conducted survey research for a professional organization based in Chicago by utilizing the Internet as a population base. I have conducted various consulting projects for nonprofit organizations in my community. Finally, I have been involved in numerous focus groups, both as a participant and as a moderator.

Greene can use some of this material to make the case that she is indeed qualified by moving it up higher in the letter. She should emphasize these qualifications rather than the fact that she hasn't worked as a market-research manager.

While I have no direct management experience, I do believe that my background of working with people, both individually and in committees, provides me with the insight needed to be a successful manager.

This paragraph provides the perfect opportunity to apply the "Turning a No into a Yes" technique described on page 12. By simply omitting the negative opening clause and making the rest of the sentence sound more confident, she makes herself a much more viable candidate for the job without being dishonest about the shortcomings in her background.

Please consider me for this position as I think I could contribute a great deal. Feel free to contact me so we can get together and discuss this further.

Greene needs to take a more proactive approach. She should not leave the ball in the employer's court. The phrases "I think I could contribute" and "Feel free to contact me" sound wimpy. Greene needs to make much stronger statements about her ability to contribute and the desirability of a meeting.

November 6, 2000

Mr. Edward Rivera
State Farm Insurance Cos.
1 State Farm Plaza
Bloomington, IL 61710

Dear Mr. Rivera:

My experience in marketing research and sales support coincides remarkably well with the details of the market research-manager position that you advertised in the *Chicago Tribune*.

I have conducted survey research for a professional organization based in Chicago by utilizing the Internet as a population base. I have managed various consulting projects for nonprofit organizations in my community. Finally, I have been involved in numerous focus groups, both as a participant and as a moderator.

My background of working with people, both individually and in committees, provides me with the insight needed to be a successful manager.

Please consider me for this position as I stand ready to make a considerable contribution. I will contact you next week to set up an appointment to meet and further discuss how my background would fit your needs.

Thank you for your consideration.

Sincerely,

Stacey Greene
Research Analyst
Spiegel, Inc.

September 10, 2000

Joe Morrison
Western Massachusetts Agricultural Research
63 North Street
Deerfield, MA 02052

Dear Mr. Morrison:

I am applying for the Germination Research Project Manager position that was advertised in the August issue of *Plant Physiologists Monthly*.

Briefly, I currently hold a Postdoctoral Research Associate position at the University of Nebraska Department of Biochemistry. My research involves the purification and characterization of a protein phosphatase from the chloroplast thylakoid membrane. This enzyme is involved in dephosphorylation of the light-harvesting complex II which may regulate the State 2 to State 1 transition in photosynthetic energy distribution.

I am very interested in the announced position and feel that I possess the qualifications listed. At the University of Kentucky and at the University of Oregon I have been responsible for the general operation of the labs that I have worked in. This work has included operating and maintaining modern biochemical laboratory equipment, training others in the use of instrumentation, analyzing and reporting research results, managing part-time student workers, complying with chemical and radioisotope safety regulations, and maintaining laboratory inventory. I have excellent communication skills and work well with people from diverse backgrounds.

Although I have not had direct experience with corn, I have had extensive experience in seed physiology. Mainly, I have been responsible for research on carbohydrate and lipid metabolism and their relationship to seed germination. This research has included the separation of soluble sugars and triglycerols and the examination of in vitro translation products from isolated poly(A)+RNA. I have also had direct laboratory experience in protein purification and immunological detection of proteins. My M.S. degree research at Duke University was part of a joint research project with MacroAgro Corporation and involved assessment of pine seedling quality using various physiological indices. In college, I took 29 credits of graduate biochemistry and plant physiology courses, I have taken 10 credits of graduate statistics courses, and have been directly responsible for field and laboratory experimental design and analysis.

You will find more information about my education and research experience in the enclosed resume. Please contact me at (402) 555-2392 during business hours, or email me at hmarker@unlinfo.unl.edu if you have any further questions. Thank you for considering me for the Germination Research Project Manager position.

Sincerely,

Harry Marker

The Problem

Many scientists, like Harry Marker, feel the need to provide a narrative of their entire career and all their scientific research. Like Stacey Greene, they need to realize that a cover letter should entice the employer into inviting the applicant to an interview and not become an autobiography of a life's work. Scientists, like other jobseekers, should relate their past experience to what they think they would be doing in the prospective job. Most scientists also enclose a detailed resume (called a curriculum vitae) that provides all the same information about their scientific endeavors, so it's superfluous to repeat that information in the cover letter. Harry's paragraphs are much too long to be easily readable.

Body of Marker's Letter, Critiqued

I am applying for the Germination Research Project Manager position that was advertised in the August issue of Plant Physiologists Monthly.

This is a fairly standard, formulaic opening for a cover letter. While there is nothing wrong with such an opener per se, it will not command the same attention as one written in a more interesting, unusual manner.

Briefly, I currently hold a Postdoctoral Research Associate position at the University of Nebraska Department of Biochemistry. My research involves the purification and characterization of a protein phosphatase from the chloroplast thylakoid membrane. This enzyme is involved in dephosphorylation of the light-harvesting complex II which may regulate the State 2 to State 1 transition in photosynthetic energy distribution.

It's obviously silly to say "briefly" when there's nothing brief about Harry's letter. He can summarize this information more concisely and save the details for his vitae. If he feels his vitae simply doesn't adequately describe his research, he might consider a supplemental sheet summarizing his research activities.

I am very interested in the announced position and feel that I possess the qualifications listed.

Harry should show the employer how he is qualified; he shouldn't just tell him. He should also eliminate the wimpy "I feel."

At the University of Kentucky and at the University of Oregon I have been responsible for the general operation of the labs that I have worked in. This work has included operating and maintaining modern biochemical laboratory equipment, training others in the use of instrumentation, analyzing and

reporting research results, managing part-time student workers, complying with chemical and radioisotope safety regulations, and maintaining laboratory inventory.

Harry could break up this long paragraph and make it much more readable by using the highlighting techniques described on page 14.

I have excellent communication skills and work well with people from diverse backgrounds.

Such a value judgment will carry much more credibility if he can attribute it to former employers and/or professors.

Although I have not had direct experience with corn, I have had extensive experience in seed physiology.

Like Stacey Greene, Harry can turn a "no" into a "yes" by omitting this negative first clause. In fact, without that clause, the sentence would be a good basis for a more attention-grabbing opening paragraph.

Mainly, I have been responsible for research on carbohydrate and lipid metabolism and their relationship to seed germination. This research has included the separation of soluble sugars and triglycerols and the examination of in vitro translation products from isolated poly(A)+RNA. I have also had direct laboratory experience in protein purification and immunological detection of proteins. My M.S. degree research at Duke University was part of a joint research project with MacroAgro Corporation and involved assessment of pine seedling quality using various physiological indices. In college, I took 29 credits of graduate biochemistry and plant physiology courses, I have taken 10 credits of graduate statistics courses, and have been directly responsible for field and laboratory experimental design and analysis.

Most of this information should be in Harry's vitae or research-narrative summary supplement. He should skip the breakdown of college credits, which doesn't belong in a cover letter.

You will find more information about my education and research experience in the enclosed resume. Please contact me at (402) 555-2392 during business hours, or email me at hmarker@unlinfo.unl.edu if you have any further questions. Thank you for considering me for the Germination Research Project Manager position.

Harry's stance is not proactive. He does not ask for an interview, but instead leaves the next move up to the employer.

Septemper 10, 2000

Joe Morrison
Western Massachusetts Agricultural Research
63 North Street
Deerfield, MA 02052

Dear Mr. Morrison:

My extensive experience in seed physiology would enable me to make a valuable contribution in the Germination Research Project Manager position that was advertised in the August issue of *Plant Physiologists Monthly.*

My responsibilities for the general operation of the labs at the University of Kentucky and at the University of Oregon align well with what you require in a research project manager:

- operating and maintaining biochemical laboratory equipment;
- training others in the use of instrumentation;
- analyzing and reporting research results;
- managing part-time student workers;
- complying with chemical and radioisotope safety regulations;
- maintaining laboratory inventory.

My previous employers can verify that I have excellent communication skills and work well with people from diverse backgrounds.

I currently hold a Postdoctoral Research Associate position at the University of Nebraska Department of Biochemistry, where my research involves the purification and characterization of a protein phosphatase from the chloroplast thylakoid membrane.

Described in detail in the enclosed vitae is my research involving carbohydrate and lipid metabolism and their relationship to seed germination, as well as my direct laboratory experience in protein purification and immunological detection of proteins. While pursuing my M.S. degree at Duke University, I worked on a joint research project with MacroAgro Corporation, which involved assessment of pine seedling quality using various physiological indices.

I'm convinced it would be worthwhile for us to meet. I will call you in two weeks to schedule an interview. If you have any questions, please contact me at (402) 555-2392 during business hours, or email me at hmarker@unlinfo.unl.edu.

Thank you for considering me for the Germination Research Project Manager position.

Sincerely,

Harry Marker

August 4, 2000

Dr. Peter Cherry
Georgia Institute of Technology
Parker H. Petit Institute for Bioengineering and Bioscience
315 First Drive
Atlanta, GA 30332-0363

Dear Dr. Cherry,

I am seeking a new position. It can be a postdoc position, or a permanent job, or something I probably do not know about. But let me introduce myself.

My name is Andrew Taylor. I am a postdoc in the lab of Dr. Michael Cohen, Technical University, Haifa, Israel. I've been working in yeast molecular genetics for many years studying, in succession, mitotic recombination, chromosome maintenance, and cell cycle. Please find details of my scientific career in my curriculum vitae which is included in the end.

My fellowship ends next April and therefore I am looking for a new position. The trick is that I am trying to change my career to a more computerized field. I am sure that Yeast Genome project is the best place for me. And I believe the project would profit from hiring me. After so many years in yeast genetics, and with my deep interest in genome organization, I know and understand virtually every bit of the related information.

My main problem is that I do not have any formal education in computer sciences, and therefore cannot prove my knowledge by presenting papers. Nevertheless, here is a more or less complete list of my computer skills.

Windows/MS-DOS	Very deep technical level. Memory management, physical and logical data organization, program interaction, batch jobs. Several times I happened to beat our computer center in retrieving "lost" data. Of course, a lot of software including Windows with applications. I can start working with a new program in no time. I simply know, or rather feel how a program should work, and usually it is correct.
UNIX	I would say I have a good working knowledge of UNIX. I can organize my environment, I know many standard UNIX programs, can, and do write simple scripts to cover my needs and for practice.
Apple	I worked a couple of times on Mac and PowerPC computers, and did not find it difficult. I was able to manage from the first moment, apparently because of my good knowledge of Windows.

Internet	This includes working knowledge of HTML, FrontPage, FTP, telnet, TCP/IP, and Usenet. I am well familiar with Java, Cobra, C++, Perl, and CGI, although I need to learn these languages and programs better.
Databases	Paradox, FileMaker Pro, DataQuip

Unfortunately, I do not have any formal training in any of these areas. This is what I badly need, and am longing for. I would be more than happy to take courses in programming, computer architecture, and the like. I love learning, and I am quick at it.

What else? I like, and I do help people when they have computer related problems. Colleagues from all our departments come to me even though my Hebrew is pretty bad, as well as their English. I am a hard worker. Usually, I spend 12+ hours a day in the lab.

To conclude, I would consider any reasonable position in the project as long as it allows my professional growth.

Thank you for your time and consideration. And sorry for the enormous length of my letter.

The best of luck,

Andrew Taylor

The Problem

Andrew Taylor is trying to make a slight shift in his scientific career to a position that is more computer-based than his previous work. While he has had considerable experience with various kinds of computers, he has neither formal training in their use nor proof of his expertise in the form of academic publications. He includes a lengthy list of his computer skills that has no place in a cover letter. In addition, Taylor commits a number of other egregious cover-letter sins. While his letter adopts a friendly and accessible tone, it rambles and is too informal in spots. He also accentuates the negative and describes what the employer can do for him instead of what he can do for the employer.

Body of Taylor's Letter, Critiqued

I am seeking a new position. It can be a postdoc position, or a permanent job, or something I probably do not know about. But let me introduce myself.

Taylor's opening is confusing and a little too informal. It also sounds as though he is willing to do *anything*. Employers prefer applicants to say exactly what they want to do and why they are qualified.

> **My name is Andrew Taylor. I am a postdoc in the lab of Dr. Michael Cohen, Technical University, Haifa, Israel. I've been working in yeast molecular genetics for many years studying, in succession, mitotic recombination, chromosome maintenance, and cell cycle. Please find details of my scientific career in my curriculum vitae which is included in the end.**

Taylor needs to condense the above paragraph and the one below to get at the highlights of his career and show how it could relate to a position with this prospective employer.

> **My fellowship ends next April and therefore I am looking for a new position. The trick is that I am trying to change my career to a more computerized field. I am sure that Yeast Genome project is the best place for me. And I believe the project would profit from hiring me. After so many years in yeast genetics, and with my deep interest in genome organization, I know and understand virtually every bit of the related information.**

Hidden within this paragraph is some good attention-grabbing information that belongs in Taylor's earlier paragraphs.

> **My main problem is that I do not have any formal education in computer sciences,**

Employers don't want to hear about what problems you will bring to the job; they want to hear how you will solve their problems. They don't want to hire people who will cost them a lot of time and money to train. Taylor doesn't need to present an entire litany of his shortcomings in his cover letter, the main function of which is to get him an interview. He can be positive and yet still be honest.

> **and therefore cannot prove my knowledge by presenting papers. Nevertheless, here is a more or less complete list of my computer skills.**

The listing doesn't belong in Taylor's cover letter (and is omitted in this critique) and it may not even have a place in his job-seeking package at all. If he is determined to use such a list, he can instead include it as a supplement to his resume.

> **Unfortunately, I do not have any formal training in any of these areas. This is what I badly need, and am longing for.**

Here, Taylor tells the employer his own needs instead of describing how he can meet the employer's needs. The employer is mostly interested in improved profitability, efficiency, and/or productivity (remember the PEP formula?); Taylor's letter should describe how he could contribute in these areas.

> **I would be more than happy to take courses in programming, computer architecture, and the like. I love learning, and I am quick at it.**

No matter how much Taylor loves to learn or how quick he is, it will still be a burden for the employer to train him or to wait for him to be trained.

> **What else? I like, and I do help people when they have computer related problems. Colleagues from all our departments come to me even though my Hebrew is pretty bad, as well as their English. I am a hard worker. Usually, I spend 12+ hours a day in the lab.**

This paragraph is unfocused and too informal, especially the phrase "What else?" The information about the language barriers in the lab is superfluous. Taylor should be aware that many employers would view the more than twelve hours a day in the lab as a negative rather than a positive; they would probably prefer someone who is more well-rounded and has a life outside the lab.

> **To conclude, I would consider any reasonable position in the project as long as it allows my professional growth.**

Again, Taylor needs to be more focused and not sound as though he is willing to do anything. Even more importantly, he must not talk about *his* professional growth but how he will contribute to the employer's growth.

> **Thank you for your time and consideration. And sorry for the enormous length of my letter.**

Instead of apologizing, Taylor should edit his letter. A good start would be to take out the computer-skills list and make it a supplement to his vitae.

Taylor also leaves the ball in the employer's court and fails to ask for an interview.

August 4, 2000

Dr. Peter Cherry
Georgia Institute of Technology
Parker H. Petit Institute for Bioengineering and Bioscience
315 First Drive
Atlanta, GA 30332-0363

Dear Dr. Cherry:

I am prepared to bring my years of research in yeast genetics and extensive knowledge of genome organization to your lab. I particularly would like to enhance your operations through my broad computer background when my current fellowship ends in April.

I am currently doing postdoctoral work in the lab of Dr. Michael Cohen, Technical University, Haifa, Israel. I've worked in yeast molecular genetics for many years, studying, in succession, mitotic recombination, chromosome maintenance, and cell cycle.

My computer knowledge comes from extensive hands-on experience with Windows/MS-DOS, UNIX, Apple Macintosh, and Internet and database software. Colleagues seek me out for my computer expertise. I have detailed my specific experience in each platform on an enclosed supplemental sheet. I am also more than willing to enhance my knowledge by taking courses in such areas as programming and computer architecture.

I am convinced that it would be mutually beneficial for us to meet. I will contact you in the near future to arrange a meeting. Should you have any questions before that time, you may reach me during business hours at the phone number shown on my vitae.

Thank you for your time and consideration.

Best regards,

Andrew Taylor

Writing-Style Guidelines

Because editing is an acquired skill, we've included a number of exercises that you can use to sharpen your writing-style editing skills before you tackle one of your own letters. Apply the checklist that follows to the exercises. Then we'll show you how we edited and rewrote the same passages.

✓ Use active voice over passive voice. The active voice leads to lively, concrete writing, while the passive voice leads to abstraction. Learn to convert weak passive sentences into strong active ones.

Weak Passive: My experience was greatly increased due to two summer internships I had.

Strong Active: The two summer internships I completed add to my experience.

✓ As suggested on page 19, use action verbs to provide a more vivid and dynamic picture of your accomplishments. Avoid weak verbs such as forms of the verb "to do," "to be," or "to work" (everyone works; use a more descriptive verb).

Nonaction: I did a number of projects for the engineering department.

Action: I performed a number of successful projects for the engineering department . . . OR I completed a number of successful projects . . . OR I developed a number of successful projects . . .

✓ Keep sentences short and concise. Brief, simple sentences keep the reader's attention. Long, wordy, and complex sentences tend to distract the reader.

Long Sentence: While completing my internship, I had the opportunity to be involved in a number of different activities, ranging from revamping the main management information system to long-range computer-needs assessment, as well as handling personnel decisions and day-to-day operations of the MIS department.

Short Sentences: During my internship I assisted in the revamping of the main information system and conducted a long-range computer-needs assessment study. I also managed the MIS department.

✓ Similarly, avoid long paragraphs. A key to your cover letter's appearance is a welcoming look, not one that appears forbidding because of lengthy paragraphs. The simple solution is to keep paragraphs to a maximum of one to two sentences. Break one long paragraph into several shorter ones. Another way to beak up your paragraphs for greater readability is to use a bullet format (see the section on highlighting, page 14).

Long Paragraph: While serving as marketing manager for Amazon.com, Inc., I developed a distribution model that increased sales by more than $200,000, I pioneered an inventory tracking system that saved the tools and hardware division more than $100,000 in lost units, and supervised the development of a ground-breaking advertising campaign. Furthermore, I was responsible for managing a staff of forty people, guiding a department budget that exceeded $1 million, and producing numerous sales and marketing reports for top management. Besides this experience, I have a bachelor's degree from Stetson University and an MBA from Harvard. As you can see, the combination of my experience and education would make me an invaluable person to head your new product division, and I would like to suggest that we schedule a meeting as soon as possible to discuss the possibility.

Short Paragraphs: While serving as marketing manager for Amazon.com, Inc., I developed a distribution model that increased sales by more than $200,000; pioneered an inventory-tracking system that saved the tools and hardware division more than $100,000 in lost units; and supervised the development of a ground-breaking advertising campaign. I was responsible for managing a staff of forty, guiding a department budget exceeding $1 million, and producing numerous sales and marketing reports for top management.

I have a bachelor's degree from Stetson University and an MBA from Harvard. My combined experienced and education would make me an invaluable person to head your new-product division.

May I suggest we schedule a meeting as soon as possible to discuss the possibility?

***Or* Bullet Format (Highlighting):** While serving as marketing manager for Amazon.com, Inc., I:
• developed a distribution model that increased sales by more than $200,000;

- pioneered an inventory-tracking system that saved the tools and hardware division more than $100,000 in lost units;
- supervised the development of a ground-breaking advertising campaign;
- managed a staff of forty;
- guided a department budget exceeding $1 million; and
- produced numerous sales and marketing reports for top management.

I have a bachelor's degree from Stetson University and an MBA from Harvard. My combined experienced and education would make me an invaluable person to head your new-product division.

May I suggest we schedule a meeting as soon as possible to discuss the possibility?

✓ **Use parallel construction.** One of the tools for making longer sentences clear and readable is to use parallel construction. Place similar ideas within your sentences and use the same grammatical construction for each.

Not parallel:	My skills include that I am a team player, hard-working, motivated, and a self-starter.

Parallel:	I am a highly motivated, hard-working self-starter, who believes in being a team player.

✓ **Avoid unnecessary words.** Pleonasms, as explained on page 47, use more words than are necessary to express an idea.

Pleonastic:	My job included developing reports on a monthly basis.

Tight:	My job included developing monthly reports.

✓ **Check for coherence.** A confusing or puzzling sentence can be a disaster in a cover letter. A sentence is coherent if all components of the sentence are logically related to all other components of the sentence.

Incoherent:	Involved in the hospital even while still in school, I developed several new procedures that the psychology department at Johnstown Hospital implemented.

Coherent:	While still in school, I developed several new procedures that the psychology department at Johnstown Hospital implemented.

✓ Check spelling and punctuation. Because most word-processing software programs are equipped with spell-checking and grammar-checking programs, job-seekers have virtually no excuse for spelling or punctuation errors. Keep in mind, however, that you cannot rely on these checkers to find correctly spelled, but misused, word forms.

Incorrect: I was highly involved in there accounting department's overhaul. Its quiet an experience to see how technology can improve efficiency—and moral to.

Correct: I was highly involved in their accounting department's overhaul. It's quite an experience to see how technology can improve efficiency—and morale too.

Editing/Rewriting Checklist

Did you . . .

✓ Change passive to active voice?

✓ Use action verbs?

✓ Avoid weak verbs?

✓ Keep sentences short?

✓ Keep paragraphs short?

✓ Use parallel construction?

✓ Avoid unnecessary words?

✓ Check for coherence?

✓ Check spelling and punctuation?

Editing Exercises

Don't forget to keep in mind not just good writing style, but all the other principles of a good cover letter!

(1) The following is an actual letter written in response to a classified advertisement. How would you improve it?

> **Currently employed as administrative assistant to one of my company's vice presidents, I am seeking employment where my secretarial, administrative and management background can be better utilized.**

Now you rewrite it: _____

_____

_____

_____

Now, here's how we would rewrite the same paragraph. Compare how you rewrote the paragraph to the way we rewrote it.

> My strong secretarial, administrative, and management background, along with the experience I've acquired as administrative assistant to one of my company's vice presidents, would enable me to make a solid contribution to Network Solutions.

Here's the second paragraph from the same letter:

> **Having graduated from the University of Indiana in June with a management degree, I believe my comprehensive relative experience and interpersonal contact I gained through extracurricular and summer job involvement has prepared me extremely well for a management position in your division.**

Now you rewrite it: _____

_____

_____

_____

Now, here's how we would rewrite the same paragraph. Compare how you rewrote the paragraph to the way we rewrote it.

My comprehensive experience and management degree from the University of Indiana have prepared me extremely well for the management training position in your division. I also gained interpersonal skills through extracurricular activities and summer jobs.

(2) The following is a letter that tries to use a clever angle. The job-seeker wrote it to a computer company. See how you can improve it.

> **In the chronology of computers, starting in the 1940s with the development of the first general purpose digital computer through the 1950s and the development of the UNIVACs through the 1960s and the development of COBOL through the 1970s and the development of fourth-generation integrated circuits through the 1980s and the development of the Macintosh computer through the 1990s and the development of super-chips and artificial intelligence and to the 2000s and beyond and the development of wireless technologies, you and your companies have been significant players in the development of the computer and the "computer age."**

Now you rewrite it: _____

_____

_____

_____

Now, here's how we would rewrite the same paragraph. Compare how you rewrote the paragraph to the way we rewrote it.

> In the chronology of computer technology, you and your companies have been significant players in the development of computers and the "information age."

Here's the second paragraph from the same letter:

> **I am writing to you because my main objective as a computer programmer is to associate with a firm that is truly in the mainstream of computer technology. At present, as you will note on my enclosed resume, I am associated with Futuristic Computers, Inc., as a senior designer and programmer. This position affords me very heavy experience in all phases of hardware and software development.**

Now you rewrite it: _____

_____

_____

_____

Now, here's how we would rewrite the same paragraph. Compare how you rewrote the paragraph to the way we rewrote it.

> My objective as a computer programmer is to contribute my skills and experience to a firm that is truly in the mainstream of computer technology.
>
> I am currently associated with Futuristic Computers, Inc., as a senior designer and programmer. Here, I've acquired considerable experience in all phases of hardware and software development.

③ The following is a letter written to a financial-services company by a recent college graduate. How would you improve it?

> **This August I will be graduating from the University of Mexico with a bachelor's degree in finance and am seeking an opportunity to use my background. I am writing to ask if you anticipate any such openings at your company in the near future.**

Now you rewrite it:_____

_____

_____

_____

Now, here's how we would rewrite the same paragraph. Compare how you rewrote the paragraph to the way we rewrote it.

> I will graduate in August from the University of New Mexico with a bachelor's degree in finance. I am writing to ask if you anticipate any openings in which I could contribute my finance background to enhance your company's success.

Here's the second paragraph from that same letter.

> **Based on my experience working part-time with a local brokerage house, I feel I would be an asset to your company. Becoming a member of your finance staff would fulfill my goal of becoming a professional and would give me the opportunity to grow as a business leader.**

Now you rewrite it:_____

_____

_____

_____

Now, here's how we would rewrite the same paragraph. Compare how you rewrote the paragraph to the way we rewrote it.

My part-time experience with a local brokerage house would be an asset to your company.

④ The following is a letter to a computer company by a recent college graduate. See how you can improve it.

I am a recent college graduate who is looking to enter the computer field. In view of my academic record (3.89/4.0), my program emphasis on computer languages, and my specific interest in computers, I strongly believe you should consider employing me in the computer pool at Apex Computers, Inc.

Now you rewrite it:_____

_____

_____

_____

Now, here's how we would rewrite the same paragraph. Compare how you rewrote the paragraph to the way we rewrote it.

I am a recent college graduate intending to enter the computer field. My curricular emphasis on computer languages combined with my strong academic record qualify me well for a position in the computer pool at Apex Computers, Inc.

Here's the second paragraph from the same letter:

Of particular interest to me is the opportunity to offer my related experience in technical and research writing, as well as my extensive education knowledge of the subject. For example, my senior-year research thesis examined how laptops with wireless technology could be used in the classroom, a project where my technical writing skills excelled. My thesis was then printed and distributed to all the professors at the university.

Now you rewrite it:_____

_____

_____

_____

Now, here's how we would rewrite the same paragraph. Compare how you rewrote the paragraph to the way we rewrote it.

> Of particular interest to me is the opportunity to offer my related experience in technical and research writing. For example, my senior-year research thesis examined how laptops with wireless technology could be used in the classroom. The thesis was deemed so good that my major professor had it distributed to the entire university faculty.

Pleonasms .

A pleonasm is the use of more words than are necessary to express an idea. Eliminate all unnecessary words. Go through your letters and cut out all extraneous words and phrases—then, go through and do it again. See below for a list of common pleonasms and how they can be shortened.

Pleonastic	Tight
in light of the fact that	since, because
for recycling purposes	for recycling
one particular youngster	one child, a child
on a daily basis	daily
a Career Fair to be held May 15	Career Fair May 15
symposium, which will be held on October 20 in the lobby itself	symposium October 20 in the lobby
during that period of time	when
at this point in time, at the present time	now (even "now" may be unnecessary)
in order to, in an effort to	to
for the purpose of	for
graphics department, which is located in the Knott Building	graphics department in Knott Building
end result	result
utilized (not so much a pleonasm as jargon)	used

Mechanics: Printing, Packaging, and Mailing

After you've polished the text of your cover letter to perfection, you need to determine how best to produce the final copy. Of course, you'll want to type it. These days, typing generally means word processing on a computer and using a printer for output. If you don't have your own computer, many public libraries have computers and most of the major office supply centers and copy shops rent time on their computers.

The Output

The key element of the cover letter you produce is a neatly printed (no smears or streaks) letter using black ink. Printing your letter on a laser printer is still the best option, but using a late-model inkjet printer should work just as well—as long as you wait for the ink to dry. Stay with black ink—we've seen too many letters from job-seekers with color printers who decide to use many of the colors as an attention-getter; these letters get attention all right, but just not in the way you want. Finally, avoid using older inkjet printers and NEVER use the now very old-fashioned dot-matrix printer.

The Font

One of the many great advantages of personal computers is an almost unlimited choice of typefaces—fonts—to use on your cover letter. Just make sure that the font you choose is not too ornate, wild, or difficult to read. Your cover-letter font must match your resume font. Some popular fonts for resumes and cover letters include New Century Schoolbook, Bookman, Palatino, Arial, Helvetica, and Times Roman. We suggest a point size no smaller than 10 point and no larger than 12; 11 point is ideal.

48

The Paper

It's best if the paper your cover letter is printed on matches your resume paper, and studies have shown that the heavier your resume paper is, the more seriously the employer will take you. For purity and simplicity, the standard is the classic white, twenty-pound 8 1/2 by 11 bond paper. If you want to fit that more serious criterion, you might try using twenty-four-pound or twenty-eight-pound bond paper. If you really don't like white, you can use one of several "neutral" colors, such as ivory, cream, buff, gray, light blue, and tan. If you're applying for a creative field, you can be a little more flamboyant in your choice of color. But here's what's not acceptable:

- **Paper of a nonstandard size.** Some job-seekers send letters on 8 1/2 by 14 paper (legal size) or 7 by 10 (monarch size) or some other odd size hoping to make their letter stand out. All you really succeed in doing with a nonstandard size is annoying the employer because your letter sticks out of the stack, falls out of the pile, or is hard to file or scan.
- **Social stationery.** It should go without saying that scents, flowers, and cartoon-decorated stationery have no place in the business world.
- **Your current company letterhead.** We once read an article that actually advised job-seekers to write their cover letters on their current employer's letterhead to prove they were employed. To an employer receiving a cover letter on company letterhead, the message is: "This person steals supplies from his company. He would probably steal from me, too."

The Envelopes

The standard #9 or #10 envelope, either white or a color and texture matching your cover letter/resume stationery, is best. If you have many enclosures, such as writing samples, lists of references, and a salary history—or if you know the employer is scanning your materials (see "Scanning," page 51)—a 9 by 12 envelope is recommended because it keeps the enclosed materials flat. By the time the person with hiring power gets your letter, however, the envelope will most likely be long gone, so it is a fairly unimportant part of your sales package.

The Perfect Package .

For the typical job-hunter, the following makes a terrific package that may impress an employer:

- Your cover letter printed on a personalized letterhead
- Your resume on a matching letterhead of the same type of paper
- An envelope in matching paper with your name and return address printed in the left-hand corner
- An attractive commemorative stamp

Please note two important aspects of the perfect package. First, all the printed elements match in terms of format, printing, and paper. Second, only a cover letter and resume are included; you should never send a salary history or reference list, unless requested to do so by the employer.

When to Mail .

When you are job-hunting using traditional methods, such as Sunday classifieds or cold-contact mailings, timing may be important. Since the best and most plentiful want ads appear in the Sunday newspaper, you are likely to be writing cover letters that day. Should you mail them right away? The answer is an unequivocal "Yes" when you are responding to a blind-box number ad, for the simple reason that the employer has rented the box for only a limited amount of time, sometimes as little as a week. For other ads, you may be better off mailing your letter as late as Tuesday so it won't get buried in the pack of letters that other job-seekers mailed on Sunday to arrive Tuesday. When we were going through ad responses, we always found we could pay more attention to the stragglers that came after the bulk of them.

One final comment about Sunday classifieds. In some cities, because parts of the Sunday paper (including the job listings) are actually printed early on Saturday, you may be able to buy the paper Saturday afternoon. In these cases, sending off a letter so that the employer receives it on Monday may give you a slight edge over other job-seekers whose letters arrive later in the week.

For cold-contact mailings, some career experts have suggested you target your letters to arrive Wednesday or Thursday, the days the power person is most likely to be at his or her desk.

Delivery Stunts

You can sometimes make an impression by having your letter hand-delivered by messenger (if the employer is in the same city) or air-expressed to another city. Neither method is cheap, but if it's the job of your dreams and there is a special reason for you to respond quickly, you may want to spring for one of these methods. If your primary motive is to impress the employer with the trouble and expense you've gone to, be aware that it may be the secretary, not the power person, who knows you used a special kind of delivery.

Some career experts have suggested you can gain an advantage by marking "Personal" or "Confidential" on the envelope and even go so far as leaving your return address off. The idea is to keep a secretary from screening your letter and to arouse the employer's curiosity. Use this technique, however, at your own risk, since many employers may be more annoyed than intrigued.

Other Delivery Methods

Some employers now ask job-seekers to fax or email their cover letters and resumes.

- **Faxing.** For best results, make sure your cover letter and resume are printed on white paper with black ink. Employers sometimes ask you to fax your materials since it's so fast and efficient, but they may also be doing it so they can scan your materials into a database. If you know the employer is scanning your materials, make sure you read "Scanning" below for tips on how to reformat your cover letter and resume.
- **Emailing.** For job postings on the Internet, employers often ask you to email your cover letter and resume. Again, the reasons are speed and efficiency, as well as the ease of entering your information into a database. For more details about job-hunting on the Internet and the proper format for emailing cover letters and resumes, see "Job-Hunting on the Internet," page 74.

Scanning

Many companies, especially high-tech companies, use document-scanning technology to quickly and efficiently match job openings with qualified job-seekers. They perform automated searches for keywords and phrases that describe the skills and education required for the position. Thus, when you write a cover letter and resume for scanning, it is extremely important to use terms and familiar industry acronyms (jargon) that describe your skills and experience.

Although many employers who scan resumes electronically don't scan cover letters, they often use cover letters to help them code the source of resumes. They want to know whether you sent your resume in response to a print ad or Internet ad, or whether you were referred to the employer's company or are simply making a cold contact. Your cover letter provides that information, so if you know the company is scanning resumes, don't omit the cover letter—it provides information that your resume can't.

Like the faxed version, a scannable cover letter should be printed with black ink on white paper—and should not be folded. The type should contain no formatting (such as bold, italics, and bullets) and no multiple columns. Both your resume and cover letter should be produced in a plain, sans serif type such as Helvetica, Futura, or Arial. You can find more about scannable resumes and cover letters in "Key Career and Job Web Sites," page 160.

Keeping a Record

It's a good idea to keep a record of every cover letter you send out so you remember each position you applied for, and know when you need to follow up with each employer. There are three easy ways to keep a record.

(1) Keep a computer file of every letter you write. Not only is this method good for record-keeping, but you'll also have your own collection of cover letters to borrow from when it's time to write new ones.

(2) Since merely keeping files of each letter you write doesn't cover other vital information you'll need handy, consider setting up a job search log such as the one found on the next page. You can make one fairly easily in a spreadsheet program (such as Microsoft Excel), or you can buy a pad of columnar-ruled paper (or just make some vertical rule lines on notebook paper). You should assign separate columns for: position you applied for, company name and address (if known), name of contact person and phone number for follow-up, date you sent your cover letter/resume, and follow-up date and notes.

(3) You can also record the history of each cover letter/resume on an index card. Make sure you record all the information about each employer and job you applied for, as described above for the job search log. Keep them in an index card box; it's too easy for loose single cards to get lost in the shuffle.

position applied for	company name and address	contact person/ telephone number	date cover letter/ resume sent	follow-up date/ notes
Customer Service Manager	Burlington County Bank 17 Main St. Haddon, NJ	Blanche White 856.555.2356	11.15.00	11.20.00 Fax Number: 856.555.2357
Branch Manager	Lindenwold Bank 183 W. Pine St. Westmont, NJ	Ralph Shuman 609.555.3544	11.25.00	11.30.00 Secretary Name: Bonnie Smith
Loan Supervisor	Smith Savings and Trust 99 Lake Ave. Clinton, PA	Amy Van Horn or John Evans 215.555.6548	11.27.00	12.02.00

Using Cover Letters Creatively

You can expand your networking opportunities by writing cover letters to organizations other than direct employers, and making other creative uses of your cover letters.

- **Letters to your college career services office.** Such letters are particularly practical after you've graduated and moved away from your college town. A well-written letter will impress the career services staff and possibly get you preferential treatment. Some career services offices also serve nonalumni. See a sample letter on page 101.
- **Letters to professional and trade organizations.** Almost all professional and trade organizations have some type of placement service, whether they make your resume available to member companies, publish situation-wanted ads in the group's newsletter, post jobs on their Web site, or run a job hotline. Sometimes there is a charge for

the service, sometimes not. You can send your resume with a nice cover letter to all the organizations in your field. Don't forget general professional organizations for women and minorities, such as the Business and Professional Women's Association or the National Association of Black Law Enforcement Officers. These same organizations are also great places to try and build your network. Find more information in "Key Career and Job Web Sites," page 160. See a sample letter on page 116.

- **Letters to employment agencies.** Employment agencies frequently advertise just as direct employers do, and it should be noted that 10 percent of job-hunters at the managerial and executive level get jobs through employment agencies and executive-search firms. You can answer their ads with a cover letter that is not substantially different from one you would send an employer. The only difference is you should acknowledge that you are applying for a position with the agency's client company. You can also write cold-contact letters to agencies, especially those specializing in your field. This method is not a particularly effective way to find a job, but in an extensive job search, it is another way to ensure you have covered all the bases. You will have considerably better luck if you follow up these uninvited letters to agencies with phone calls.

- **Letters to executive-search firms.** Job-seekers generally don't seek out search firms; instead, executive-search firms rely on contacts in the business world to refer candidates who will fill the needs of their client companies. These companies usually keep search firms on retainer. However, it never hurts to send your resume to an executive-search firm, especially if you can use the referral-letter approach. See a sample letter on page 115.

- **Sending a letter without a resume.** Some experts suggest you send a letter without a resume because when employers see a resume with a letter, many assume you are unemployed and sending similar mailings to a number of people. If you can summarize relevant highlights of your experience in a letter so well-written that the employer will want to talk with you further, you may be better off not sending a resume. That way your correspondence will seem more like a business letter than the run-of-the-mill resume mailing, just like the hundreds of others that cross the employer's desk. You can ask for a meeting instead of an interview.

- **Responding to a hidden opportunity in an ad.** You might see an ad for a position you're not qualified for, but you can see a hidden opportunity in the ad. For instance, one woman saw an ad for a museum-director position that she did not qualify for, but since it was in the natural-history field, where she did have considerable experience, she wrote a letter suggesting she would make a great assistant to the new director. She got the job. The same thing worked for another woman when she saw an ad seeking people to sell advertising space for a new magazine. She wasn't interested in selling, but she knew that after some ads were sold, the

magazine would need an editorial staff. She wrote offering her editorial services, and she, too, was successful in creating a position for herself.

- **Informational interviews.** Use your cover letter to ask for an informational interview. While this technique is especially effective if you are a new graduate unsure of the type of job you want or are switching careers, it can work for all job-seekers by uncovering the hidden job market. The technique is simple. Introduce yourself in your letter and, instead of asking for a job interview, ask for a small amount of the employer's time for an informational interview. While you might have to wait a while for an appointment, most employers are happy to oblige since they know you don't plan to talk them into hiring you—and because people love to talk about themselves.

  At the interview, find out as much as possible about the company and its operations, needs, plans, and challenges. Find out about the kinds of positions within the company and what plans might be afoot for either expansion or downsizing. Leave your resume if it seems appropriate, but don't be pushy. You will then be armed with all the information you need to target the company with an uninvited letter in the future. You may even be able to use that letter to propose a new position after you've identified a need within the company, based on the information gathered during your interview.

  Yours won't exactly be a cold-contact letter, because now you know someone important in the company. Whether the company has an opening or whether you propose a new position, the employer will be much more likely to consider hiring you because he or she has already met you. You are a known quantity. The informational interview is also a great networking tool because even if the employer doesn't have an opening, he or she may refer you to someone who does.

  A great source for much more information about networking, and specifically informational interviewing, is another of our books, *A Foot in the Door* (Ten Speed Press). See also the sample letters asking for an informational interview on pages 102 and 103 of this book.

- **Seeking consulting and freelance opportunities.** You can use your cover letter as the job-seeker on page 133 has—to solicit freelance and consulting assignments. A direct-mail campaign seeking these kinds of opportunities is an excellent networking tool, and freelance assignments always have the potential to turn into full-time jobs. If nothing else, these assignments will keep food on the table while you look for a full-time position.

- **Zapping your cover letter into cyberspace.** Every day, more new job-finding opportunities are opening up on the Internet—Web sites where you can post your resume, search for jobs, and network electronically. See "Job-Hunting on the Internet," page 74.

Sticky Issues

Salary Requirements

What if an ad asks for salary requirements or history? The request for salary requirements is a common problem in the writing of cover letters, especially responses to blind-box ads. Employers often use blind-box ads as a way to screen out applicants who want a bigger salary than the company feels it can or wants to pay. At the other end of the spectrum, employers sometimes eliminate from consideration those who ask for a salary much lower than what the position pays. Instead of being viewed as a bargain, the low-priced applicant is often considered to be at a lower level than the kind of person the employer seeks. The employer asks you to put your salary requirement in your cover letter, and if you want too much or too little money, you probably won't get called for an interview. You don't know who the employer is, so there's no reason for the company to bother sending you a polite rejection letter.

If salary is the most important issue to you, you have no problem. You can put your salary requirement in your cover letter with no qualms because if the employer eliminates you as too expensive, you will have lost nothing because you don't want to work for less than your required salary anyway.

If, however, the job itself is important to you and you are flexible about salary, you have more of a problem. The ad description sounds like the perfect job for you. You really want it, but the ad asks for a salary requirement. If you put down your ideal salary, you risk being eliminated from a job you'd love to have.

Your choices:

- You could skirt the issue entirely by either leaving out the salary requirement or addressing it with a sentence such as: "My salary requirement is negotiable," or: "I am earning the market value for a systems analyst with four years of experience. I would be happy to discuss my compensation requirement in an interview." Be aware that some advertisers include a disclaimer that no applicant will be considered without a salary requirement. Research shows, however, that many—if not most—employers will still consider you if you omit the salary requirement. (The studies indicate that few applicants ever hear from a company that absolutely insists on a salary requirement.) Since you are "damned if you do and damned if you don't," you might as well take the approach with which you are most comfortable.

- You could state your current salary and say it is negotiable. "I am currently earning an annual salary of $35,000, and my salary requirement is negotiable." Then it's up to you whether you're willing to accept a lower salary.

- You could give a range, for which the low-end figure is 10 percent above your current or last salary.

An employer who asks for a salary history is trying to determine the size and frequency of raises you are accustomed to. You run the same risks providing a salary history as you do with a salary requirement. If you decide to include the history, do it on a separate sheet of paper so you won't take up space in your cover letter.

References

Should you include references in your cover letter? No. References belong in the interview phase of job-hunting, so they should not be listed in your resume or cover letter. Occasionally, an ad will specify that you must send references. In that case, you should list them on a separate sheet rather than take up precious space in your cover letter. You can, of course, refer to the sheet in your letter. ("A list of references is enclosed.")

Letters of Recomendation

Should you send letters of recommendation? Generally speaking, no. Letters of recommendation have little credibility because anyone who would write you a letter of recommendation wouldn't say anything negative about you.

Negatives in Your Job History

Should you explain negative aspects of your job history? Another tough question. In the beginning of this book, we said the cover letter is an opportunity to explain the negatives. However, we must caution you to give careful thought to bringing up any negatives. (See "The Domino Effect," page 68.) Most negatives are better handled in the interview, and you can wait for the employer to bring them up instead of calling attention to something they might not have noticed.

Chances are, whatever "problem" you think might exist with your job history is much more of an issue to you than to the prospective employer. There is no point in making your problem the employer's problem. When in doubt, leave it out.

Don't say anything about not having enough experience. Make the most of the experience you do have and let employers judge for themselves. Take advantage of your transferable skills (see page 13).

If any negative circumstances surrounded your leaving a past job, don't mention them. One letter we received got off to a horrendous start by telling the employer in the first sentence that the applicant was fired from his last job. What a turnoff.

It is probably not necessary to point out a lack of educational qualifications. One letter-writer wrote the following plea for consideration despite her lack of a college degree (which was included in the ad as a job requirement): "Will you consider someone with the qualities you are looking for and great experience but less than four years of college?"

We believe the writer would have been better off omitting that sentence. She could have let her otherwise good cover letter and fine resume stand on their own merits. If the employer was impressed with her experience, he might not have even looked at her educational background. If he liked her letter and resume, he might have decided that a degree really wasn't essential for doing the job.

It can't hurt to briefly explain why you are making a career switch, especially if you are making a radical shift from one field to another. The sample on page 104 shows an effective way to explain career shifts.

Follow-up Letters

Follow up is crucial in the job search process. Very few job-seekers write follow-up letters of any kind, thus you can stand apart when you follow up with a thank-you letter, a letter acknowledging a rejection, a declining letter, or an acceptance letter.

Post-Interview Thank-You Letters

Terrific. You got an interview. Now, the minute you get home, do not pass Go, do not collect $200. Instead, sit down and write a thank-you letter to the employer while the interview is fresh in your mind. And if you interviewed with more than one person, make sure you write a thank-you letter to each one. If you know the employer is planning a quick decision, you may want to make special arrangements to have your thank-you letter delivered quickly, such as hiring a messenger service or even hand-delivering the letter.

Thanking a prospective employer for his or her time is just common courtesy. But, a thank-you letter can do more:

- It's a way to keep your name in front of the employer.
- It's a way to build on the strengths of the interview and emphasize the match between you and the job, especially now that you know more about the company and the position.
- It's a way to bring up anything you thought of after the interview that is pertinent to the employer's concerns.
- You may be able to address anything that went badly in the interview and try to correct it—but be extremely careful.
- If the employer has asked you to send additional materials that you didn't bring to the interview (such as references or writing samples) you can include a thank-you letter with the items.
- It's a way to restate your understanding of the next step in the process. ("I look forward to meeting with your vice president, Mrs. Green, sometime next week.")
- It's an opportunity to restate your interest in and enthusiasm for the job.
- It's another chance to show how well you express yourself.

But the best thing about thank-you letters is that, even though virtually every book on job-hunting advises sending thank-you letters, very few job-seekers actually do so. If you're one of the few that do, you're bound to have an edge.

See sample thank-you letters beginning on page 153.

Rejection Letters .

When you get a rejection letter—without an interview or after an interview—write back to thank the employer for acknowledging your letter or thank him again for the interview. Encourage the company to make good on its promise to keep your resume on file. The employer will be impressed with your courtesy and continuing interest. You'll keep the dialogue going with the company, and your name will more likely be remembered the next time there's an opening.

Sample Follow-up to a Rejection Letter

April 19, 2000

Ms. Suzanne Lee
Rehabilitation Hospital
10 Medical Court
St. Louis, MO 63188

Dear Ms. Lee,

Thank you for your letter dated April 17th. I am disappointed that because of the reorganization of the department the medical records clerk position is no longer available.

I appreciate your offer to keep my resume on file. I am very interested in working for a leader in medical care such as Rehabilitation Hospital.

Once again, thank you for your time and consideration. Good luck with the reorganization, and I hope to hear from you in the near future.

Sincerely yours,

Deborah S. Stiles

Declining Letters

You got a job offer! But, alas, you've decided the job is not right for you. The money isn't right, or another offer is better. Write a nice letter turning down the job. You never know when you might need that employer again, so you want to stay in his or her good graces.

July 9, 2000

Mr. Jerry Fine
American Graphics
12 West 15th Street
New York, NY 10050

Dear Mr. Fine,

Thank you for all the time you and Ms. Atwood spent considering me for a position as a graphic artist. I sincerely appreciate your consideration—as well as that of your staff members who spent time with me during this process.

I most appreciate your offer of employment; however, after much deliberation and careful analysis, I must respectfully decline your offer. I feel another opportunity better matches my qualifications and career path.

This decision has been very difficult; yours was an outstanding opportunity.

I hope our paths will cross again in the future. You have been most kind, and I again thank you for your time and consideration.

Sincerely,

Michelle A. Barton

Acceptance Letters

It's the moment we've all been waiting for! You got an offer, and it's the perfect job! You've decided to go for it. Congratulations!

It's important to write a letter thanking the employer, and accepting the offer. The most important reason to write an acceptance letter is to state your understanding of the terms of employment: salary, benefits, starting date, probationary period (if any), duties, and so forth. That way, if there is any discrepancy between your understanding and your new employer's, it can be brought out in the open before you start work. It's also a written document that may help if legal difficulties ever arise.

September 6, 2000

Ms. Lisa T. Wallace
Eastman Kodak
343 State St.
Rochester, NY 14650

Dear Ms. Wallace,

Thank you for your telephone call of September 4 offering me a job as a chemical engineer with your processing department at an annual salary of $45,000. Please consider this letter my formal acceptance.

As I mentioned to you, because I am a group leader in a major experiment with my present company, I will not be able to start until the middle of October.

The offer fulfills one of my career goals: working for Kodak.

I want to thank you for all your help and consideration. I also appreciate the help of Dr. Maddox and Mr. Lustig.

Please let me know if you need any additional information or if there are details I should be aware of prior to my arrival in October.

Cordially,

Jessica P. Hopps

Cover Letter Hall of Shame

We hope we've taught you in the preceding pages everything you need to know to write a great cover letter. If you're still unclear about how to distinguish an effective letter from one bound for the circular file, we offer some additional characteristics of an inferior cover letter, followed by two samples of what not to write—the two worst cover letters we've ever seen.

Characteristics of an Ineffective Cover Letter

Sometimes the best way to know how to write a strong, attention-getting cover letter is to examine elements of a poor one as we've done in the following list. It's a sure bet that your cover letter won't get much attention if:

☑ **Its opening paragraph is boring and formulaic:**

- "In response to your advertisement in the National Ad Search, September 10, 2000, please consider my resume in your search for a Mechanical Engineer".

- "I am seeking a full-time position in which I may use my prior work experience. I would be interested in exploring the possibility of obtaining such a position with your company as a Research Scientist".

- "Please find enclosed a copy of my current curriculum vitae, list of publications, statement on teaching philosophy and experience, and a summary of research interests for your consideration for a faculty position in cell biology."

Ho hum. Although a typical cover-letter opening, such as those above, is not wrong, it is simply not as effective as one that makes the employer sit up and take notice.

☑ **It is more than one page, or the paragraphs are too long and deadly to be readable or inviting.**

☑ **You try to write your autobiography instead of a sales letter that entices the employer to call you in for an interview.**

☑ **You dilute the power of your sales message with such phrases as "I believe" or "I feel."**
Note how much stronger the sentence below is without "I feel."

Before:	With this broad-based background I feel that I have the necessary skills to contribute significantly to your organization's success.
After:	With this broad-based background, I have the necessary skills to contribute significantly to your organization's success.

☑ **You ask for an entry-level job.**
If you're a new college graduate, chances are you may end up in an entry-level job. But why advertise what sounds like a lack of ambition?

✓ You make unsubstantiated value judgments about yourself.

There's nothing wrong with saying: "I'm extremely well-organized and a hard worker." Consider, however, how much more power such a statement has if you can substantiate it through professors or former employers: "Any of my previous employers can attest to the fact that I'm a well-organized hard worker." (Be sure they really can attest to those attributes!)

✓ You dwell on what the employer can do for you instead of what you can do for the employer.

Before:	I feel that a post at your center would enable me to widen my experience and achieve several of my career goals.
After:	I would like to contribute my experience and assist the center in reaching its goals.

✓ You include an unsolicited salary request.

✓ You include unnecessary and negative information.

One job-seeker had written three wonderfully effective paragraphs. With the fourth, suddenly his letter fell apart: "My most recent experience was with a wood-furniture manufacturer. The firm was experiencing financial difficulties when I joined them. Unfortunately, the requisite external financing could not be arranged, resulting in the firm being closed. Prior to that, I had been with an apparel manufacturer that downsized its operations."

He should have asked himself whether the negative information added anything to his sales message. Too often, job-seekers try to tell their entire career sagas in the cover letter, sparing no detail. Remember that your letter should offer a taste—an appetizer, and a good one at that. Your resume provides a little of the meal, while the interview is the place for the full banquet that is your career—including any less-than-savory aspects.

✓ You sound too desperate—as though you are willing to do anything.

One job-seeker wrote: "Feel free to copy and distribute my resume to any other personnel who may be interested in me." Such a statement is a turnoff for employers. They have much more respect for applicants who know exactly what they want to do and how they can make a contribution.

☑ You don't know enough about the company to which you're writing.

A biologist included this line in his letter: "If your corporation is involved in molecular research or biological production, I encourage you to consider me for an opening." Most employers expect applicants to know whether the company to which they're writing offers the kind of job the applicant seeks.

☑ You are too wimpy and passive about your past experience.

Don't use such phrases as "I was taught" or "I was given the opportunity." Say "I learned" and "I took the opportunity."

The Two Worst Cover Letters We Ever Saw.

We're not sure what it means that both of these letters were sent to radio stations. The letter that follows arrived on shiny corrasable paper, typed in faded gray ink, complete with sexist salutation, misspellings, typos, sentence fragments, and nothing that a good cover letter should contain.

Radio WHRS
34532 Highway 22
Harrisburg, PA 17103

Gentlemen:

I am a recent graduate of Harrisburg College; In which I received a Bachelor of Arts Degree in Communications. And I would very much like to persue a caree in media.

I have enclosed a copy of my resume for your review. I would appreciate it very much if you would look it over to see if I meet your standards for employment with your radio station.

I would also appreciate hearing on your decision on employment with you. One thing I can promise is that I will Give 100% to my job. Since WHRS is my hometown radio station, I only want to hear thes on it.

Thank you.
Very Truly Yours,

Gilbert David King

This one was in response to a classified ad seeking an ad copywriter for a radio station. Is this guy serious? As if the letter weren't bad enough, the sample he sent bordered on pornographic.

Randy Ricci
1601 Washington St.
Tacoma, WA 98000

I am currently a paint salesman. I have previously worked as the manager of a frankfurter restaurant and as a market researcher.

I am also a writer. I've written about fifty short stories and two short novels. I read a lot and have some knowledge of current events. Enclosed is a sample from one of my novels.

I'm a creative guy. Maybe, I could be a copywriter.

Randy Ricci

Checklist

Your cover letter is ready for mailing! Or is it? Use this checklist to see whether you've written the most dynamic letter possible.

☑ Is it an original letter rather than a mass-produced copy?

☑ Is it addressed to a named individual (unless it is a response to a blind ad)?

☑ If it's a response to a blind ad, is the salutation nonsexist?

☑ Does the letter grab the reader's attention in the first paragraph?

☑ Is it confident without being arrogant?

☑ Have you left out everything negative?

☑ Is the letter neat and attractive?

☑ Is every word spelled correctly? Is all grammar, syntax, punctuation, and capitalization correct? Is the letter free of typographical errors?

✓ Is it no longer than one page?

✓ Is the letter concise and to the point?

✓ Does it avoid such clichés as "I have taken the liberty of sending my resume enclosed herewith"?

✓ If it's in response to an ad, does the letter speak to the requirements of the position?

✓ Is it interesting?

✓ Does it project the image of a person you would like to get to know better if you were the employer? Have you read it from the employer's perspective?

✓ Have you told the employer what you can do for him rather than what he can do for you?

✓ Have you presented your Unique Selling Proposition?

✓ If you're a recent grad, have you avoided relying too much on an academic frame of reference?

✓ Have you avoided pleading for favors?

✓ Have you avoided getting too detailed?

✓ Have you spelled out what kind of job you're looking for?

✓ Have you avoided rewriting your resume in your cover letter?

✓ Have you avoided describing your personal objectives in vague terms?

✓ Have you avoided listing hobbies or interests unless relevant to the position?

✓ Have you listed accomplishments?

✓ Is it clear where the employer can reach you during business hours? Have you ensured that either a person or a machine will take the employer's call?

✓ Have you used action verbs?

✓ Have you requested action and told the employer you'll call for an appointment?

✓ Is the letter free of the wimpy phrases, "I feel," "I think," and "I believe"?

✓ Have you signed your name boldly and confidently?

The Big Picture

No matter how wonderful and dynamic your cover letter, if you don't fully understand the job process, you will have problems finding a job and end up frustrated or disappointed with your efforts. To help you master the process, we've included the following sections: The Domino Effect, Marketability, Networking, Sources of Hidden Job Opportunities, and Job-Hunting on the Internet.

The Domino Effect

If you overlook one element in your job search, the pieces will not fall into place, and you may not get the job you want. The five key dominos include:

1. Marketing preparation. Preparation is perhaps the most important element of any successful job search. The strength of your preparation will carry you through the entire job search process. Preparation includes:
   - determination of your strengths and weaknesses
   - evaluation of your job and career interests
   - establishment of a career track/path
   - analysis of geographic areas of interest
   - research on companies of interest
   - networking with anyone who might be able to provide you with job leads (more on networking in the next section)

2. Your dynamic cover letter. You're an expert on writing a dynamic cover letter by now, right? Use all the examples and resources in this book!

3. Your excellent resume. A resume is a document that describes your work experience, your education and any special training, and your skills. What makes an excellent resume, however, is marketing. You have to consider yourself a product, with the employer as the buyer...why should the employer buy (hire) you? Your resume is a key marketing tool in your employment search. And to help you develop an excellent resume we've included the names of the top resume books in the "Recommended Reading" section, page 163, as well as some great Web sites in "Key Career and Job Web Sites," page 160.

④ Interviewing skills. No matter how introverted you may be, you can learn to interview well. It simply takes learning some basic rules and then practicing and refining your technique as much as possible. And to help you polish your interviewing skills, we've included some of the best interviewing books in the "Recommended Reading" section, page 163, as well as some great Web sites in "Key Career and Job Web Sites," page 160.

⑤ Follow-up. This last domino is as important as the first; if you don't follow up and follow through you might not be successful in your job search. Follow-up includes:
- calling employers and asking for an interview
- returning phone calls
- writing thank-you letters to anyone who has helped you in your search or with whom you have met
- writing acceptance or declining letters to job offers

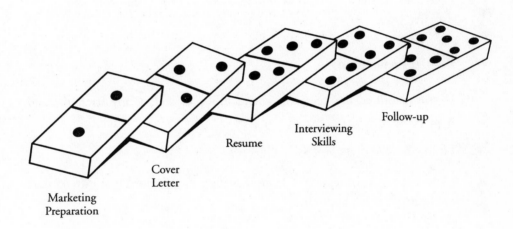

Marketing Preparation · Cover Letter · Resume · Interviewing Skills · Follow-up

Marketability

The more you strive to improve your marketability, the more effective your job search will be. Keep in mind that marketing yourself to potential employers is central to the search. Employers will rarely seek you out because of *who* you are, so seek them out and present yourself in a manner that will inspire them to hire you. That's what marketing is all about—promoting a product, which in this case is *you*. The job search is no time to be modest; tout your accomplishments, your skills, your education. Don't be afraid to toot your own horn in your cover letter. Job-hunting is also not the time to be disorganized or unprepared; develop a plan and follow through. As a starting point, test your marketability with the following quiz.

Test Your Marketability

Answer "yes" or "no" to the following statements and then check your score when you're done.

Part I: Personal and Professional Development

(1) I read newspapers and magazines (including trade journals) and visit industry Web sites regularly to stay abreast of key issues in business and my field of interest. (Y) (N)

(2) I have the appropriate education and experience for the kind of job I am interested in attaining. (Y) (N)

(3) I attend classes, seminars, and workshops that will add to my knowledge and expertise. (Y) (N)

(4) I belong to at least one professional organization. (Y) (N)

(5) I have had increasing levels of responsibility and/or been promoted in the past five years. (Y) (N)

Part II: Preparation

(1) I have identified my key skills and abilities, as well as my strengths and weaknesses. (Y) (N)

(2) I know how to dress professionally. (Y) (N)

(3) I know the key elements (my Unique Selling Proposition) that differentiate me from other job applicants. (Y) (N)

(4) I know exactly the kind of job I want next. (Y) (N)

(5) I can research companies and industries. (Y) (N)

Part III: Networking

(1) I keep in contact with colleagues I have met at professional events. (Y) (N)

(2) I keep in contact with people I have gone to school with or worked with in the past. (Y) (N)

(3) I attend professional conventions and make contacts with leaders in my field. (Y) (N)

(4) I introduce myself to others at social and business functions. (Y) (N)

(5) I exchange business cards (or networking cards) with all new people I meet at these functions. (Y) (N)

Part IV: Cover Letter Essentials

1. I have developed and honed, and can communicate, my Unique Selling Proposition.   (Y)   (N)

2. I address all my cover letters to named individuals (except when answering blind-box classified ads).   (Y)   (N)

3. I never leave the ball in the potential employer's court; I always take a proactive approach.   (Y)   (N)

4. I state what I can do for the employer rather than what the employer can do for me.   (Y)   (N)

5. I have eliminated all errors from my cover letters, and printed them on standard business paper using a high-quality printer, or followed the do's and don'ts of sending email cover letters.   (Y)   (N)

Part V: Resume Necessities

1. I have identified two or three key accomplishments for each job I have had.   (Y)   (N)

2. I have determined my best format (chronological, functional, or some combination of the two) for my resume.   (Y)   (N)

3. I have used strong action verbs in my descriptions.   (Y)   (N)

4. I have eliminated all errors from my resumes and printed them on standard business paper, using a high-quality printer, or followed the do's and don'ts of sending email resumes.   (Y)   (N)

5. I have produced a resume that stands out from other resumes.   (Y)   (N)

Now total your answers. If your "yes" answers total:

    24–25, you're in great shape.

    21–23, you need some fine-tuning.

    18–20, you need more preparation.

    Under 18, you have a lot of work ahead of you.

Networking

As we've already mentioned, career experts estimate that the vast majority of job openings are never advertised or publicly announced, but filled through other avenues, such as word of mouth—or networking—as well as cold contacts. The likelihood of a job opening not being advertised at all increases with the level of the job. Yet, even with this knowledge, most job-seekers fail to fully utilize networking for all it's worth.

Networking means developing a broad list of contacts—people you've met through various social and business functions—and using them to your advantage when you look for a job. People in your network can give you job leads, offer you advice and information about a particular company or industry, and introduce you to others so that you can expand your network. And, of course, members of your network are a key component of referral cover letters.

How do you develop a network? The best place to start developing your network is with your family, friends, and neighbors—and with their family, friends, and neighbors. But don't stop there. Talk to coworkers, colleagues in your industry, and those you meet at industry gatherings, such as trade shows and conferences. Talk with former coworkers, bosses, and teachers.

The key to successful networking is deciding to put in the energy needed to make it work. First, you need to get organized (for example, keeping a business card file or computer database). Second, you need to stay in contact (for example, through regular phone calls, email, and holiday greetings). Third, you need to set goals for yourself (such as "making five new contacts per week").

You'll find much more information about networking online (see "Key Career and Job Web Sites," page 160) and in print (see "Recommended Reading," page 163).

Sources of Hidden Job Opportunities

Your newspaper, business magazine, trade journal, or favorite Web site contains more than just job ads to help in your job search. (Don't forget that a company's Web site and annual report are often the best sources for these kinds of leads.) Here are other stories to look at when developing a list of contacts for your search:

- Stories about products or services in great demand. Companies with hot products may be looking to expand their work force. You may get in on the ground floor by writing a dynamic cover letter to the company before the firm advertises for more workers.

- Your knowledge of technological breakthroughs, new patents, discoveries, and other developments in an industry or occupation can make a big impression in your letter, especially if you can catch on to the trend before anyone else does.

- Most business sections in both business/trade magazines and newspapers run a column listing promotions, retirements, and sometimes terminations and resignations. The departing person may create an opening you could fill.

- Contract awards. When a company successfully bids on the right to manufacture goods or perform services for another company or the government, chances are the company that won the contract will need more workers.

- Major events—such as a world's fair or Olympic Games—create openings for companies located in the host city, and for companies providing goods or services to the event.

- The opening of a new plant or facility can create opportunities.

- Reports of increased sales and earnings, which can be found not only in external publications but also in the company's own annual report, may signal workforce expansion.

- Is the corporate headquarters moving to your city or state? Undoubtedly the firm will need local people to fill openings.

- Mergers and acquisitions can create opportunities because many workers leave the affected companies in the face of an uncertain future.

- Stock underwritings and IPOs of new and developing companies may foretell opportunities because capital will now be available to fill openings and create new positions.

- Articles on meeting speakers and award-winners can provide fodder for dynamic cover letters.

Source: Adapted from Jack Erdlen, Vice President, Romac International; Wellesley, Massachusetts.

Job-Hunting on the Internet

No job-hunting book published today would be complete without some discussion of strategies and sources of job-hunting on the Internet. The Internet is an increasingly important component of a comprehensive job search, but you should not make it the only one. A good rule of thumb, say most career experts, is that the Internet portion of your job search should consume no more than a quarter of the total time spent. However, if you're in a highly technological field—especially one related to computers—spending additional time on the Internet portion of your search will probably prove productive.

Note: Web addresses for all of the specific resources mentioned below are provided in "Key Career and Job Web Sites," page 160.

How do you begin? You'll need access to the Internet and an email account. If you have a computer at home, you can get both by signing up with one of many fee-based services (such as America Online, EarthLink, MSN Internet, and AT&T) or free services (such as NetZero and Juno). If you don't have a computer at home, you can still job-hunt on the Internet, as many public libraries and specialized retail outlets (cyber cafes) offer Internet access. You simply need to get a free Web-based email account (such as one from MSN HotMail or Yahoo! Mail).

Once signed up for Internet access and an email account, most job-seekers start their online journey by going to one of several career development Web sites, such as Quintessential Careers—yes, that's our site—or The Riley Guide. These sites can help you to develop or hone your resume and cover-letter writing; find the best sources for researching companies; strengthen your interview skills; learn how to network; master salary negotiation; and perfect other key career and job-hunting skills.

Once you've honed your career-development skills, the next step is actually looking for a job. There are many specialized job and career Web sites (such as for college graduates, executives, minorities, etc.) as well as general job sites, and—depending on who you are and where you are in your career—chances are you'll find some specialized job sites you'll want to explore.

Keeping these issues in mind, there are four different types of Web resources for job-seekers:

(1) Job-networking Web sites and discussion lists. Web sites such as Industry Insite provide a place for professionals seeking work in your industry to network and share information. Thousands of Internet-based discussion lists are also available on almost every subject and profession imaginable. Join one or more of these lists and network with people in

your field; employers sometimes subscribe to these lists so they can screen potential candidates. Finally, many professional organizations have Web sites that provide forums to facilitate networking.

(2) General job databank and resume sites. Web sites such as HotJobs.com, CareerShop.com, and FlipDog.com have large databases of job openings that you can search by profession or keyword. A complete list of the best of these sites can be found at Quintessential Careers: The Best Job Resources. College students should visit College Recruiter or JobDirect. A complete list of the best of these sites can be found at Quintessential Careers: College Grad Resources. Many of these sites allow you to post your resume for free, and some even offer job and applicant matching services. Some of these sites also allow you to post your resume without revealing your name for the sake of confidentiality.

(3) Specialized job sites. There are hundreds of specialized job Web sites, from employment recruiters of all types to specialized job databank sites that focus on a specific industry. If you're an executive, you might want to go to 6FigureJobs.com. If you're an accountant, try AccountingJobs.com. And if you're a marketer, visit MarketingJobs.com. You'll find a list of the best of these specialized job sites at Quintessential Careers: Career and Job-Hunting Resources by Industry.

(4) Company sites. If you would most like to work for a specific set of companies, the best solution might simply be to go to each company's Web site and review job postings. Many of these companies allow you to apply online, and they often list the contact person so you can easily follow up, as you would after sending a traditional cover letter and resume to an employer.

One last caution: Just remember that the Internet is not some magic place where everyone finds a job, so don't have undue expectations—and don't abandon all the traditional methods of job-hunting, either.

About email cover letters: When you send a cover letter electronically, your opening paragraph becomes even more important. If your letter is not a grabber, all an employer has to do is press the Delete key.

Here are the other keys for cover letters sent via email:

- Keep it brief; even shorter than a standard cover letter.
- Know the company guidelines, which usually can be found on each company's Web site.
- Make the subject line of your email specific to the job you are applying for, but don't waste it either. Instead of making your subject line "Job 345-23ABEW," add your USP to it: "Dynamic sales manager in response to Job 345-23ABEW."

- Send your message as Plain Text—without formatting such as italics, bold, or bullets—rather than HTML. Not everyone can read messages in HTML format; Plain Text also makes your words easier to scan. Choose this option in your email program's settings.
- Make good use of keywords.
- As always, edit and proofread your work, making sure there are no errors of any kind.

Cover Letter Quiz

So, you're a cover letter pro by now—are you sure? Test your cover-letter knowledge by responding to the following questions to the best of your ability. For multiple-choice questions, choose the best response. Here's one quiz where it's OK to "cheat"; feel free to refer back throughout this book for the answers.

The Quiz

① What will a good cover letter get you?
— A document to go with your resume
— A job
— Lots of praise
— An interview

② Which of the following is *not* a function of a cover letter?
— Telling the employer what kind of job you seek
— Showing how well you write or express yourself
— Describing what you expect to get from the job you're applying for
— Enticing the reader to want to get to know you better by interviewing you

③ When should you send a cover letter?
— Only when an ad specifically requests it
— Every time you send out your resume
— When you need to list your salary requirement
— When you need to list references

4. Which of the following is *not* one of the three types of cover letters?
  .___ The Referral Cover Letter
  .___ The Uninvited/Cold Contact Cover Letter
  .___ The Hot Prospect Cover Letter
  .___ The Invited Cover Letter

5. What job-hunting technique does the highly effective Referral Cover Letter spring from?
  .___ Networking
  .___ Prospecting
  .___ Cold-canvassing
  .___ Interviewing

6. True or false: The effectiveness of taking risks with the opening paragraph of your cover letter depends greatly on the field/industry in which you are seeking a job.
  .___ True
  .___ False

7. Which of the following is *not* one of the three most common cover letter mistakes?
  .___ Leaving out salary requirements
  .___ Not addressing the letter to a named individual
  .___ Failing to be proactive; leaving the ball in the employer's court
  .___ Telling what the employer should do for you rather than what you can do for the employer.

8. True or false: Employers like candidates to express a willingness to perform any available job
  .___ True
  .___ False

9. True or false: Transferable skills should be mentioned in the resume only, *not* in the cover letter.
  .___ True
  .___ False

10. The fact that very few job-seekers demonstrate their knowledge of the company in their cover letters means that:
  .___ It's an incorrect practice
  .___ It's hard to research companies
  .___ You will stand out if you do demonstrate such knowledge
  .___ They are not really interested in the job

(11) True or false: It's a bad idea to include bullets in a printed cover letter because it makes the letter too much like a resume.

- ___ True
- ___ False

(12) A postscript (P.S.) on your cover letter...

- ___ Should never be handwritten
- ___ Will be the first thing the employer notices on your letter
- ___ Should be avoided
- ___ Should avoid mentioning your USP

(13) Your USP is your:

- ___ Unilaterally Simplistic Paradox
- ___ Unequaled Sexual Prowess
- ___ Unique Selling Proposition
- ___ Unforgettably Superior Popularity

(14) True or false: Long paragraphs are expected in cover letters so job-seekers can elaborate on their qualifications.

- ___ True
- ___ False

(15) True or false: It is still considered perfectly acceptable in the business world to use a salutation such as "Dear Sirs" or "Gentlemen" in your cover letter.

- ___ True
- ___ False

Checking Your Answers: Check your answers and read our explanations. Then come back and see what your score means.

Scoring: If you correctly answered . . .

14–15 of the questions: You are nearly a cover-letter expert.

12–13 of the questions: You should reread those sections of *Dynamic Cover Letters* covering topics for which you gave wrong answers.

Fewer than 12 of the questions: You need to go back and read *Dynamic Cover Letters* more closely!

Adapted from the Quintessential Careers Cover Letter Quiz. The full quiz (47 questions) can be found at http://www.quintcareers.com/cover_letter_quiz.html. Used with permission.

The Answers

① What will a good cover letter get you?

An interview. Think of your cover letter as a sales letter. Closing the sale means asking for an interview. Read more about the role of cover letters on page 1.

② Which of the following is *not* a function of a cover letter?

Describing what you expect to get from the job you are looking for. Never tell the employer what the company can do for you; tell what you can do for the company.

The other three responses *are* possible functions of a cover letter: *Telling the employer what kind of job you seek* (don't leave 'em guessing); *showing how well you write or express yourself* (because written and verbal communications skills are important in so many jobs); and *enticing the reader to want to get know you better by interviewing you.*

Read more about cover letter functions on page 1.

③ When should you send a cover letter?

Every time you send out a resume (with a few rare exceptions, such as when an ad specifies "resumes only"). Read more about general cover letter issues on page 7.

④ Which of the following is *not* one of the three types of cover letters?

The Hot Prospect Cover Letter.

The *Uninvited/Cold Contact Letter,* the *Referral Letter,* and the *Invited Letter* are all types of cover letters.

Read about the three types of cover letters on page 2.

⑤ What job-hunting technique does the highly effective Referral Cover Letter spring from?

Networking. Read more about referral letters and networking on page 6.

(6) True or false: The effectiveness of taking risks with the opening paragraph of your cover letter depends greatly on the field/industry in which you are seeking a job.

True. You can be more creative in a creative field, such as advertising, or with a more laid-back industry, such as Internet companies. Risky openers are especially risky in conservative industries, such as banking and law. Read more about cover letter openers on page 9.

(7) Which of the following is *not* one of the three most common cover letter mistakes?

Leaving out salary requirements. Salary requirements should *never* be included unless they're requested, and even then, proceed with caution.

Failing to address the letter to a named individual, failing to be proactive in your last paragraph, and *telling what the employer can do for your instead of what you can do for the employer*—all of these are *major* cover letter blunders.

Read other cover letter "do's and don'ts" on page 17.

(8) True or false: Employers like candidates to express a willingness to perform any available job.

False. You need to be very specific about what you want to do, not just say you'll do anything. Don't leave the employer guessing what you want to do. Read more cover letter strategies on page 8.

(9) True or false: Transferable skills should be portrayed in the resume only, *not* in the cover letter.

False. Portrayal of transferable skills is just as important in a cover letter as in a resume. Read more about transferable skills on page 13.

(10) The fact that very few job-seekers demonstrate their knowledge of the company in their cover letters means that:

You will stand out if you do demonstrate such knowledge. Read more about how to research companies on page 5.

⑪ True or false: It's a bad idea to include bullets in a printed cover letter because it makes the letter too much like a resume.

> *False.* Bullets can also work well in a cover letter. They can make your letter more reader-friendly. Read more about cover letter formats on page 15.

⑫ A postscript (P.S.) on your cover letter . . .

> *Will be the first thing the employer notices on your letter.* It can be a great formatting device that will attract attention. Read more about formatting tricks on page 15.

⑬ Your USP is:

> *Your Unique Selling Proposition.* Read more about your USP on page 11.

⑭ True or false: Long paragraphs are expected in cover letters so job-seekers can elaborate on qualifications.

> *False.* It's always easier on the reader to make your letter as concise as possible. Read more about the body of a cover letter on page 11.

⑮ True or false: It is still considered perfectly acceptable in the business world to use a salutation such as "Dear Sirs" or "Gentlemen" in your cover letter.

> *False,* of course. You don't want to be sexist and disregard half the population. Read more about salutations on page 8.

Cover Letter Honor Roll

Every sample letter that follows is one that received an A rating from us. With identities of writers changed to protect privacy, the samples are all based on real letters. We're sure you'll find many good ideas for your own cover letters within these samples.

Recent Grad Letter

Cold-contact letter.

Strong use of specific skills in his opening paragraph.

He does a good job of explaining how he can help the company.

B.J. Johnson
250 College Heights #22
Jupiter, FL 33458
Ph # (561) 555-5487

September 11, 2000

Mr. Fred Leiter
Ford Motor Company
American Rd.
Dearborn, MI 48121

Dear Mr. Leiter,

My solid, hands-on experience in CAD, designing ICs and layouts, and extensive knowledge of hardware description languages (VHDL, Verilog) and analog simulation software (SPICE) would provide me with the opportunity to excel in a design capacity with your firm.

The courses I have taken have prepared me well for a position in the Digital/Hardware/ASIC and VLSI/Architecture fields. I have also conducted research in design and implementation of Broadband cross-point switching fabric. I am well aware that your company does high-quality work in these areas.

My previous employers can attest that I am not only organized and detail-oriented, but I also work well under pressure and on deadline. I work well with a variety of people.

I am immediately available for employment and am prepared to relocate either domestically or overseas.

I am confident that my qualifications are an excellent fit with the needs of your company and that it would be worthwhile for us to meet. I will contact you in ten days to schedule an interview. Should you wish to contact me before that time, you may reach me during business hours at 561-555-5487. Thank you for your time and consideration.

Sincerely,

B. J. Johnson

Recent Grad Letter

The applicant requests a meeting with the campus recruiter,• but also indicates willingness to meet outside that context.

The letter targets a specific position. •

Jamie Jones
3335 NW 39th Terrace
Gainesville, FL 32606
(352) 555-1009

August 21, 2000

Mrs. Rita Pugh
Target, Inc.
777 Nicollet Mall
Minneapolis, MN 55402

Dear Mrs. Pugh:

Having been employed previously by Target, Inc., I know firsthand that your corporation is a strong and growing institution in which I could make a valuable contribution, using management and marketing experience garnered through both education and experience.

My solid educational background coupled with retail experience can only profit your corporation. That's why I'm writing to arrange an interview when your campus recruiter visits the University of Florida on September 13. I understand you will be recruiting for several candidates for your management training program.

My experience in other retail outlets has broadened my perspective and provided me with a strong customer-service orientation. I possess a clear understanding of inventory-control procedures and am adept with many computer programs used in the retail field.

Mrs. Williams, although I certainly want to meet with your recruiter when he or she comes to my campus, I would also be willing to interview for this position before that time. I'll give you a call next week to see which route you feel is preferable. If you'd like to contact me, my number is (352) 555-1009.

Thanks so much for considering me.

Sincerely,

Jamie Jones

Recent Grad Letter

Requesting a meeting with a campus recruiter is a good way to get a jump start on a post-college job search.

Gary Frey
5465 Ferguson Avenue
Pittsburgh, PA 15213
412-555-4349

This applicant makes the most of his collegiate experience.

September 15, 2000

Anne Mach
Director, Human Resources
Minnesota Mining and Manufacturing Company
3M Center
St. Paul, MN 55144-1000

Dear Ms. Mach:

My technical background, demonstrated leadership skills, and ability to meet the needs of the customer would enable me to make a valuable contribution in a chemical-engineering position at the Minnesota Mining and Manufacturing Company. Thus, I am writing to request a meeting with your campus recruiter when he/she visits Carnegie Mellon University on Oct. 24. I will graduate from the Carnegie Institute of Technology at Carnegie Mellon University with a bachelor of science degree in chemical engineering in May 2001.

I am currently a community adviser—the senior-most position in the residence-life office, with 248 people under my direct or indirect supervision—demonstrating my leadership ability. Previous employers can tell you that, because I am highly independent and responsible and because I enjoy dealing with people, I have consistently been promoted to levels of greater responsibility.

My ability to function as both a leader and a team player would enable me to serve the company well in a project-management capacity. My professors can confirm that I have acted as a team player in many academic work-group situations. In design and lab courses, my roles as leader and team member have involved collaboration, delegation of work, scheduling deadlines and meeting them, making group decisions, and sharing the leadership role. I am well experienced in gauging and improving group dynamics.

The challenging and competitive academic program I've taken has included such unique courses as photochemistry, process controls, process engineering and design, and unit operations laboratory, all of which would be particularly useful in the chemical-engineering area, especially in project management.

Ms. Mach, I will call you the week of October 9 to arrange an appointment with your campus recruiter. In the meantime, I would appreciate receiving additional information on employment opportunities and a job application form. Thanks very much for your consideration.

Very truly yours,

Gary Frey

Recent Grad Letter

Sunny DeMoss-McCann
55 Davis Hall
University Park, PA 16802
(814) 555-8729

February 24, 2000

Mr. Gene VanGemert
VP, Information Technologies
Procter & Gamble
1 P&G Plaza
Cincinnati, OH 45202

Dear Mr. VanGemert:

Your employee, Jennifer Fiester, suggested I contact you about a programming position with Procter & Gamble. As a senior student expecting a bachelor of science degree in computer science from Pennsylvania State University, I am ready to make a meaningful contribution to the P&G team.

Both my academic career and employment experience have prepared me well for a career in programming. I have been trained in developing, designing, integrating, and documenting various application programs, and programming using IBM Mainframe and UNIX operating systems. The many programming classes I've taken have taught me several different programming languages, including C++, Java, Pascal, COBOL, Assembly, and Standard ML.

My previous employers can affirm that they have entrusted me with major responsibilities and that I have adapted quickly to each of my positions. For example, as head manager at Sam's Food Market last summer, I exclusively managed the store, delegated work for employees, wrote and developed an inventory control system, and handled daily cash flow.

In addition, my position as a social director for my club at the university has helped me further enhance my communication skills.

Because you undoubtedly realize that a letter and resume can convey only a limited sense of a person's qualifications, I am sure it would be productive for us to meet in person so I can explain my credentials more fully.

I will contact you in ten days to arrange a meeting. Should you wish to reach me before that, my number is (814) 555-8729. Please leave a message if I am not available. I look forward to meeting with you. Thank you for your time and consideration.

Sincerely yours,

Sunny DeMoss-McCann

Recent Grad Letter

Note the effective opening paragraph. •——————

He adds power to his self-appraisal by citing •——————
employers and professors.

Kurt Mayer
65443 Providence Blvd., #96
Detroit, MI 48207
313-555-5621

October 4, 2000

Mr. Joseph Oliker
Human Resource Department
Whirlpool Corporation
2000 N. M-63
Benton Harbor, MI 49022-2692

Dear Mr. Oliker:

Having worked in service-based organizations, I know how valuable good employees are. All organizations, after all, have access to the same information, the same suppliers, and the same consumers. The organization that differentiates itself by effectively recruiting, training, managing, and retaining its people is best equipped to succeed in today's competitive business environment.

My desire to contribute to a company's competitive edge has motivated me to study organizational psychology as an undergraduate student and pursue an MBA focusing on human-resource management. I would like to put my knowledge and experience to work for you.

The financial, managerial, program development, and leadership skills I have gained through both employment and extracurricular experience would enable me to make a significant contribution to your organization's success. My previous employers and professors can verify that these skills, combined with my coursework, motivation, and determination to succeed, will make me a valuable asset to your organization.

I would like to have the opportunity to meet with you and discuss how I could enhance your company's success. I will contact you the week of October 16 to arrange a meeting. Should you wish to reach me in the meantime, you may call me at 313-555-5621. I appreciate your time and consideration.

Sincerely,

Kurt Mayer

Recent Grad Letter

Nell Bannister
2364 South Woodland Blvd.
DeLand, FL 32720
(904) 555-5531

February 18, 2000

Ms. Jane Sutherland
Bank of America
100 N. Tryon St., 18th Fl.
Charlotte, NC 28255

Dear Ms. Sutherland:

My training in marketing and my experience in the banking industry parallels the requirements of Bank of America's Consumer Banker Associate Program. I have recently graduated from North Carolina State University, and I am eager to put my education to work in banking.

The experience I gained in my summer jobs in banking would be a genuine asset to Bank of America. In the Fleet Merchant Services Department, I learned valuable communication skills and a professional attitude. As a loan processor for Central Florida Mortgage Company, I took the opportunity to learn how loans are processed and how relationships between agents are established and maintained. I also developed problem-solving and decision-making skills; by the end of the summer, I worked in the cash-claims analysis department making loan-foreclosure decisions.

Having worked as a computer-lab assistant while putting myself through college, I also have well-developed computer skills and a familiarity with many of the most popular software programs.

Ms. Sutherland, I am confident that it would be worthwhile for us to meet. I will give your secretary a call on Wednesday, February 23 to schedule an appointment. Should you have any questions about my interests or qualifications in the meantime, please feel free to call me at (904) 555-5531.

I thank you for considering me for the Consumer Banker Associate Program and look forward to meeting with you.

Sincerely,

Nell Bannister

Recent Grad Letter

Paul D. Koblenzer
1038 Glenwood Path
Tallahassee, FL 32308
U.S.A.
(850) 555-3211

August 27, 2000

Torsten Jonsson
Personalavd
SAS
161 87 Stockholm
Sweden

Dear Mr. Jonsson:

My education and experience in marketing and international business, as well as my fluency in English, German, Spanish, and Italian, would enable me to contribute significantly to a global accounts position with Swedish Airlines. I would be interested in employment anywhere in the world.

I will graduate this December with a bachelor of science degree in marketing from Florida State University, where I was president of the International Business Society. I demonstrated solid skills in marketing research and promotion during my experience at the Bureau of International Trade and Development at the Florida Department of Commerce, which would enable me to sell the airline's services worldwide. I also developed considerable facility with computers.

As a member of a U.S. foreign service diplomat's family, I have acquired a unique view of the international business scene, numerous cross-cultural skills, and adaptability. I am well traveled and have lived in a wide variety of international locales.

I am eager to advance the success of your company, and I am convinced that it would be advantageous to set up a meeting with your American human-resources representative. I plan to contact the American office in two weeks to arrange such a meeting. Should you desire to contact me in the meantime, I can be reached at (850) 555-3211.

Thank you for your consideration.

Sincerely,

Paul D. Koblenzer

Recent Grad Letter

Effective use of a professor referral. •

She presents a strong Unique Selling Proposition •
in her second paragraph.

Isabel Loprieno
485 Oak Lane
Tequesta, FL 33469
(561) 555-2435

June 27, 2000

Mr. Jerry Proboski
Federated Insurance Company
1890 Semoran Blvd., Suite 273
Winter Park, FL 32792

Dear Mr. Proboski:

Dr. Randall Scott of Stetson University suggested I contact you regarding the position you and he discussed in the Insurance Trainee Program of Federated Insurance Company.

I am a May 2000 graduate, but I am not a typical new graduate. I put myself through school by selling radio advertising and serving in a customer-service capacity in an art gallery.

All my jobs during my college years enhanced my formal education and provided considerable practical experience in sales and marketing, which would enable me to make a real impact as a trainee with Federated. I also participated in a number of university-sponsored marketing research projects.

As Dr. Scott can verify, my education and practical experience, coupled with my maturity and marketing skills, will be an asset to your firm.

I am enthusiastic about a career in insurance and am willing to relocate for your training program.

I will follow up this letter with a phone call next week. Thank you for your consideration.

Sincerely,

Isabel Loprieno

Recent Grad Letter

Demonstrates knowledge of the company.

Makes an effective connection between her retail-sales experience and her outside-sales career goal.

Heather Barker
2838 E. Michigan Avenue
Maplewood, NJ 07040
(973) 555-2872

March 20, 2000

Dr. Jill Fenimore
Director of Pharmaceutical Sales
Merck & Co., Inc.
1 Merck Dr.
Whitehouse Station, NJ 08889

Dear Dr. Fenimore,

Since I work in the pharmacy field, I am aware of your company's reputation in pharmaceutical research and sales. My solid background in the retail pharmacy business, along with the skills and experience that accompanied my education, should be of interest to you. My ability to communicate well with physicians and pharmacies in selling pharmaceuticals would allow me to make a difference at Merck.

I will receive a bachelor of business administration degree in marketing from Stetson University this May. Throughout my academic career, I have cultivated my special interest in pharmaceutical sales through my studies of professional selling. I would now like to draw on those abilities as a professional in the field.

I am confident that my knowledge and abilities would be of value to your company. I would like to request a few minutes of your time to discuss my qualifications. I will contact you soon to arrange a meeting. If you have any questions in the meantime, please do not hesitate to call.

Thank you for your time and consideration.

Sincerely,

Heather Barker

Recent Grad Letter

Uses of the referral technique. •————

A deft blend of academic and internship experiences. •————

Katharine Knight
2104 Pinhorn Drive
Bridgewater, NJ 08807
(732) 555-9208

October 1, 2000

Ms. Sharon Weickel
Director of Human Resources
Saks Fifth Avenue
500 Fifth Avenue
New York, NY 10022

Dear Ms. Weickel:

I'm writing to follow up on a phone conversation you had with Dawn Avant, the Rutgers University assistant director of career services, about the retail management-trainee position you expect to have available in May 2001. I've developed a strong foundation in retail, I am highly customer service-oriented, and I stand poised to bring my skills to your fine organization.

My retail experience includes an internship with your Short Hills store, as well as summer and seasonal positions with various specialty stores and boutiques.

I've also developed my abilities to lead and influence people through a long record of activities at my university. Combined with my major coursework in marketing, my secondary focus in communications has enabled me to hone my skills in interacting productively with people.

I am convinced that I am particularly well suited to meet the challenges of this position and to provide top performance in retail management. At your convenience, I would like to arrange a time for a personal interview, and I will call you in ten days to set up such a meeting. Should you wish to reach me before then, please call (732) 555-9208.

Thank you for your time and consideration.

Sincerely,

Katharine Knight

Recent Grad Letter

Uses of the referral technique. •

He presents a good approach to parlaying •
an interest into a career.

Jason Jay Johnson
108 North Lincoln Blvd.
Omaha, NE 68132
402-555-7154

October 9, 2000

Mr. Gavin Nehemiah
Omaha Snow Devils
400 E. Icy Lane
Omaha, NE 68130

Dear Mr. Nehemiah:

Dr. Patrick Oliphant suggested I write to you about your opening in the advertising and promotion department with the Omaha Snow Devils.

As an experienced athlete and a marketing major, I have played a major role in numerous fund-raisers. I also hold a part-time position as a customer-service assistant in a supermarket while pursuing my degree and playing on the college baseball team. I've worked as an assistant coach for summer baseball clinics held on my campus.

My interest and skills in sports marketing are a good match with the requirements of the position you have open.

I am convinced that we should meet to discuss how I might contribute to the team's visibility and box-office success. I'd like to phone you during the week of Oct. 23 to arrange such a meeting. You may also contact me at 402-555-7154.

Thank you, Mr. Nehemiah, for appraising my candidacy for this position.

Very truly yours,

Jason Jay Johnson

Recent Grad Letter

The applicant is writing to a manager who once hired him for what turned out to be a lengthy series of summer jobs and internships. The manager has now moved on to another company, so the applicant is writing to him to ask him to consider hiring him again.

Scott H. Hood
56 Green Lake Ave., #94
Madison, WI 53716
(608) 555-8225

May 1, 2000

Mr. John Randall
Vice President of Marketing
Lands' End, Inc.
Lands' End Ln.
Dodgeville, WI 53595

Dear Mr. Randall:

Six years ago when you hired me for my first job, I wonder if you realized that the work would become a career. Since those early days, I have advanced with Pass, Forte & Blacker to work in the departments of Catalog Control and Creative Marketing.

From this experience, I have become an expert on the intricacies of nonstore retailing. I helped spearhead a computer tracking system that allowed us to develop a relationship marketing program that, in only the first two years of operation, has increased sales by 35 percent. Furthermore, I have solid sales experience, as well as logistics experience. I know I can apply these skills at Lands' End and help continue your strong sales gains.

I want to thank you for giving me that first opportunity to explore retail, not only because I enjoy the work so much but because I've learned enough to know that I want to make a long-term commitment to this field. I have built on my retail experience with market-research consultation work.

Mr. Randall, it was such a pleasure to work with you in the past; I look forward to the opportunity to do so again. I'd like to meet with you to discuss the possibilities, and I'll call you soon to set up such a meeting. I can be reached at (608) 555-8225.

Thanks again for the career boost and for considering me a second time.

Sincerely,

Scott H. Hood

Recent Grad Letter

Note the powerful opener. •—————

She effectively demonstrates her accomplishments. •—————

Mercedes Moser
600 Rolling Acres Road
Stonybrook, NY 11790
(516) 555-2236

April 5, 2000

Mr. Lloyd Langford
United Technologies
1 Financial Plaza
Hartford, CT 06103

Dear Mr. Langford,

Could you use a scientist or field technician who gained experience in the successful operation of a large-scale ($2 million annual budget) aerospace project while still a college undergraduate? I am just such a scientist, and I would like to enhance the success of an aerospace technology firm such as United Technologies.

I hold a bachelor of science degree in aerospace science from Yale University, where my academic focus was in flight systems. I utilized the knowledge gained from my coursework to complete a one-year thesis on aerospace dimensions related to a new helicopter design concept. Not only did I refine my skills at working independently, but I also learned how to effectively communicate with and obtain information from colleagues working in my area of research. My thesis and course work provided significant exposure to experimental design techniques, statistics, technology, and proper design procedure.

My aerospace experience led to various projects with both a senior aerospace professor and the director of Yale's Department of Aerospace Studies and Applied Sciences. I am confident of my ability to successfully complete the tasks with which I would be confronted at United Technologies.

Although I am interested in gaining exposure to all types of aerospace technologies, I am particularly enthusiastic about working on projects that involve pushing forward into new frontiers of aerospace.

I know that your corporation seeks motivated, responsible individuals, and I would very much like to meet with you to discuss my possible employment. Please permit me to phone you late next week for an appointment. Meanwhile, please feel free to contact me at (516) 555-2236. Thanking you for your consideration, I look forward to meeting with you soon.

Sincerely,

Mercedes Moser

Recent Grad Letter

Uses the self-referral technique. •

Follow-up on a phone conversation. •

She makes the most of her collegiate experience. •

Note the informal greeting: it is okay to use an •
employer's first name only if the recipient has
told you to. Otherwise, it's a **big** mistake.

Katlynn P. Morgan
1540 Republic Drive
Orlando, FL 32819
(407) 555-4947

August 13, 2000

Ms. Debra Carroll
Verizon Communications
1095 Avenue of the Americas
New York, NY 10036

Dear Debra,

It certainly was a pleasure to speak with you recently. You'll find that my proven track record in sales and marketing makes me the ideal candidate for the sales position we discussed in your regional sales office in Tampa.

I was a first-place winner in personal selling at the DECA National Convention in 1999. I have continued this record of excellence in my college career with a recent national award from the American Marketing Association. My proficient oral and writing skills, as well as my natural ability to work well as a team player, make me a valuable and productive employee.

I am a well-rounded student, as you will notice on my resume. I have both participated and held leadership positions in various extracurricular activities. I am a hard worker, and my enthusiastic personality and positive attitude make me an excellent coworker.

I am convinced that you will find my qualifications strong enough to justify an interview to explore mutual interests. I will be calling you in a week or so. Should you need any additional information, please contact me. Again, Debra, thanks for your consideration.

Sincerely,

Katlynn P. Morgan

Recent Grad Letter

Seeks a student-teaching position. •

Demonstrates genuine dedication to the profession. •

Dexter Mulkey
287 21st Street
Irvington, NJ 07111
(973) 555-2132

October 17, 2000

English as a Second Language Coordinator
Essex County School Board
380 Main Street
Newark, NJ 07070

Dear Coordinator:

As a student in the Teaching English to Speakers of Other Languages program at SUNY Stonybrook, I seek a school district where I can have an impact as I do my student teaching in the spring semester of 2001. As a student teacher, I will give as much to my students and mentor teacher as I will learn from them.

I have four years of experience working as a teaching assistant in the Sussex County school system at all grade levels during the summer and university holidays. I have substituted in many different schools, including an alternative high school for students at risk of dropping out of school and those with drug and alcohol problems, and the adolescent psychiatric ward of a hospital. These experiences in difficult situations have proven I have the stamina to be an effective teacher under various conditions.

In addition to completing all the courses required by the university and the state for KP12 TESOL certification, I have taken two semesters of ESL teaching practicum and a class in methods of teaching foreign languages. My required and elective course work, combined with my experience, have prepared me to be an effective teacher, and I am confident that I am better prepared than many other student teachers.

I'd like to meet with you to discuss the ESL student-teaching positions that are available in your district. I will stop by your booth at the teacher-recruitment fair next month to set up a meeting. If you need to reach me in the meantime, please call (973) 555-2132.

Sincerely,

Dexter Mulkey

Letter Requesting a Summer Job

Good use of skills and ambition in opening paragraph. •——

She is proactive in her closing. •——

Vera L. Jones
4501 Beach Street, #A45
Daytona Beach, FL 32127
(904) 555-4528

April 3, 2000

Ms. Angel Holm,
The Gap Store Manager
The Voluisa Mall
1700 W. International Speedway Blvd.
Daytona Beach, FL 32114

Dear Ms. Holm,

My previous experience in fashion retailing, my current retail marketing education at Daytona Beach Community College, and my desire to pursue a management position in retail, make me an ideal candidate for a summer job at the Gap.

The Gap has been a retail industry innovator, in terms of product lines as well as advertising and promotion. I want to be a part of your store's success, and I know that the contribution of my experience, education, and motivation to succeed will make me an asset for your store.

I would like to request a meeting with you to discuss employment opportunities. I will contact you in the near future to arrange a time. Should you have any questions before that time, you may reach me at my home number listed above.

Cordially,

Vera L. Jones

Letter Seeking a Summer Internship

Sandy Taffida
P.O. Box 134
Piscataway, NJ 08855
(732) 555-2922

March 22, 2000

Mr. James Julia
VP, Human Resources
Honeywell International Inc.
101 Columbia Rd.
Morristown, NJ 07962

Dear Mr. Julia,

As a Rutgers engineering student in my junior year studying electrical engineering, I am seeking a summer internship in the Central New Jersey region in which I can make a genuine contribution.

My experience in retail electronics, as well as my desire to pursue research and development, have convinced me that electrical manufacturing is an option I would like to explore.

More importantly, an internship with Honeywell would be mutually beneficial. Your company has an excellent reputation for quality, and I know that the combination of my experience, education, and motivation to excel will make me an asset in any department in which you place me.

I am sure that it would be worthwhile for us to meet. I will contact you within a week to arrange a meeting. Should you have any questions before that time, you may reach me during business hours at (732) 555-3000, or at my home number listed above.

Sincerely,

Sandy Taffida

Letter to a College
Career Services Office

Alisa Baxter
38209 East Oil Lane Drive
Houston, TX 77254
(281) 555-3280

June 5, 2000

Ms. Barbara Bluebonnet
Placement Office
University of Texas
Austin, TX 78712

Dear Ms. Bluebonnet,

I am a recent graduate of the University of Texas and am in the job market for a position in nursing. My specialty is in pediatric nursing.

I am hoping that you will keep my file current and inform me when any nursing recruiters are on campus for interviews or when you hear of openings in my field.

Enclosed is an updated version of my resume for your files. Also please note my new address and telephone number for your records. I would also like to submit a resume for your electronic database and will call you for specific instructions.

Thank you so much for your help.

Sincerely,

Alisa Baxter

Letter Requesting an Informational Interview

Cody Barbara Bucher
108 Hilltop Way
Redwood City, CA 94065
650-555-2891

March 6, 2000

Mr. Steve Dascher
Sales Manager
Trinchero Family Estates
100 St. Helena Hwy. South
St. Helena, CA 94574

Dear Mr. Dascher,

I am a student at Stanford University, in the process of completing my junior year in the School of Business. The California wine business has fascinated me ever since my first trip to the Napa region. Your company has an outstanding reputation—some attribute the major growth of wine consumption in the United States to your Sutter Home brand.

I would appreciate the opportunity to meet with you briefly and discuss the California wine business, and specifically the Trinchero Family Estates. I would greatly appreciate any insights you can give me.

I will contact your office the week of March 20 to set up a mutually convenient time for this informational meeting.

Thanks so much for your time and consideration.

Sincerely,

Cody Barbara Bucher

Letter Requesting an Informational Interview

Good approach for a career changer looking for information.

Lisa Lively
3428 Talamas Drive SE
Clemson, SC 29631
864-555-3483

June 26, 2000

Ms. Jane Wilson
Director, Human Resources
General Electric Company
3135 Easton Turnpike
Fairfield, CT 06431-0001

Dear Ms. Wilson:

As an aspiring human resources manager, I have been impressed with what I've learned about GE. Your company's reputation for cutting-edge human resources programs that put employees first has inspired me to request a brief informational interview with you. I was especially interested to read that GE was rated "one of the best companies to work for" by *Fortune* magazine.

I am completing graduate work in human resources management at Clemson University after years of a career in sales. I would very much like to talk with you about your work.

Because of the obvious geographical obstacles, an in-person meeting is not practical, so I'd like to interview you by phone or email.

I'll contact you the week of July 10 to see if we can set up a time for a phone or email discussion. I will ensure that the interview does not take more than thirty minutes of your valuable time.

Thanks so much for considering this request.

Best regards,

Lisa Lively

Career Change Letter

Judith C. Beverly
7392 West University Way, #870
Austin, TX 78747
(512) 555-2933

July 28, 2000

Ms. Amy Michaels
Dell Computer Corporation
1 Dell Way
Round Rock, TX 78682

Dear Ms. Michaels,

My varied customer service and training experience, along with my extensive educational background, make me an ideal candidate for a position with Dell as a corporate trainer.

My supervisors at the Texas United Way and Austin Chamber of Commerce, where I most recently served as a volunteer trainer/facilitator, will attest to my natural abilities to plan, organize, and lead groups of all sizes.

Much of my previous work experience has been in customer service, and the tools and techniques I have learned from this industry apply directly to the skills corporate trainers need: speaking effectively, facilitating group discussion, solving problems, developing rapport, organizing, meeting goals, and managing groups.

My extensive educational background—a bachelor's degree in marketing, with minors in human resource management and communications, and postgraduate work in teaching and counseling—will help me add new perspectives and ideas to your department.

I know I can be a key player on your training team, and I would like the chance to prove that to you in an interview scheduled at your convenience. I will call you during the second week in August to schedule a meeting, but feel free to call me sooner at the number listed above. I look forward to meeting you.

Thank you for your time and consideration.

Sincerely,

Judith C. Beverly

Referral Letter

Libby Samuels
238A Cloudy Sky Drive
Seattle, WA 98103
(206) 555-3728

September 15, 2000

Ms. Jill Sabovsky
FileNET Corporation
3565 Harbor Blvd.
Costa Mesa, CA 92626-1420

Dear Ms. Sabovsky,

Your colleague Jack Southerly and I have been talking about how my skills might fit at FileNET Corporation. He said he'd discussed with you the possibility that I might assist you with some projects, so I wanted to introduce myself, and tell you a little of what I've done since working with Jack at InfoSource.

I got my master's degree at Antioch University, Seattle, in whole systems design for organizational change. Since then I've been consulting for organizations on a variety of planned-change projects. While working for InfoSource, I designed and facilitated a series of goal-setting and evaluation meetings to implement the firm's gain-share plan. I have worked with the local YWCA to design and conduct board planning retreats, and I facilitated a series of sessions for Cruel World, Inc., to develop their company mission statement.

The applicable skills in all of these projects are the ability to (1) lead groups in effective work sessions, (2) design processes that accomplish the appropriate tasks, and (3) communicate in a way that draws out the group's combined knowledge.

I'm looking for a position where my talents can be fully engaged. Jack made it clear that the decision to hire an assistant is yours, and that any position would have to go through the normal posting process. I simply wanted to let you know I'm eager, and hope to find a fit at FileNET Corporation.

I will be arriving in Costa Mesa around the second week in October. I don't yet know my local number or address. If you don't have an opportunity to call me before September 30th, I'll get in touch on my arrival. Thanks for your consideration.

Sincerely,

Libby Samuels

Referral Letter

Mark R. Shaw
1545 Elmont Street
Kansas City, MO 64114
(816) 555-3829

November 30, 2000

Mr. C. Benjamin Riley
Sprint Corporation
2330 Shawnee Mission Pkwy.
Westwood, KS 66205

Dear Mr. Riley,

Nanette Newell tells me that you are looking for a motivated employee for the job of Customer Service Representative. I have the background and the personality to excel in this position.

I have extensive, high-energy customer-service experience, and I desire to make customer service my life's work. I have frequently called upon my ability to communicate effectively, handle customer problems quickly and personably, and succeed in high-stress situations.

In addition, I have excellent organizational and writing skills, as my former employers can describe. I am currently training to enhance my IBM computer skills, and I have the desire and competence to learn quickly.

I know you won't regret giving me an opportunity to show you what I can do. I am very interested in working for your company, and I am confident that you will be happy with my performance.

I will call you in a few days to explore what the next steps will be.

Sincerely,

Mark R. Shaw

Referral Letter

Sally Radellio-Webb
2114 Galloway Drive
Manhattan, Kansas 66502
(785) 555-3743

June 23, 2000

Mr. William J. Douglas
West Educational Publishing
620 Opperman Drive
St. Paul, MN 55164-0779

Dear Mr. Douglas,

Our mutual acquaintance, Dr. Dorothy Lederhaus, with whom I am working as a postdoctoral research associate in the department of Management Science, suggested I contact you to describe the contribution I might make in research and development or product/process development at your organization.

I have a strong background in engineering and mathematics at both the undergraduate and graduate levels. The skills in management science I attained through course work, research projects, teaching experience, and pilot plant experience would enable me to analyze ecosystems and develop new ecology-friendly products.

In addition to my research experience, I coauthored two successful grant proposals resulting from my Ph.D. research.

With my background in management engineering and science, and research experience, I am confident of my ability to meet your requirements.

Please review my qualifications and see if you agree that we should meet personally. I will call you during the week of July 10 to arrange a meeting. If you desire any additional information, I can be reached at (785) 555-3743.

Thank you for considering my qualifications.

Sincerely,

Sally Radellio-Webb

Self-Referral Letter

Follow-up on a meeting at a trade show/convention. •———————

The congratulatory sentence is nice touch. •———————

Colleen Bucholtz
1245 University Blvd.
Tallahassee, FL 32308
(850) 555-0790

February 20, 2000

Mr. Morris Fiondella
Fiondella & Associates
908 Adelphi Lane
Austin, TX 78727-4111

Dear Mr. Fiondella:

I very much enjoyed meeting both you and Dan Belcher at the Performance Summit '99 in Tampa. Congratulations on your selection as Production Coordinator/Manager of the Year for your work with Mariah Carey.

My experience as a production assistant, my proven organizational skills, and my flexibility to travel would all be solid assets in a tour-production position with Fiondella & Associates.

I am thoroughly familiar with the operation of concert halls through numerous part-time and volunteer production-assistant positions in which I worked on concerts featuring Britney Spears, the Backstreet Boys, and Sheryl Crow, as well as for the Jacksonville Jazz Festival.

I have also honed my organizational skills and ability to adapt to a variety of management styles during two years as an administrative assistant.

I am widely traveled, both in the United States and abroad, and I work well on the go.

My previous employers can vouch for my ability to organize, coordinate, and make things happen. I'm sure we could both benefit from another face-to-face meeting in which I would further describe my potential contribution in a tour-support position. I will call your office during the week of February 28.

Thank you for your time and consideration.

Sincerely,

Colleen Bucholtz

Self-Referral Letter

Follow-up of a phone conversation. •

She effectively relates her experience •
to the job requirements.

Jill Berry
233 West 99th Terrace
Kansas City, MO 64114
(816) 555-2231

November 22, 2000

Continuing Education
Attn: Sean Ginger
College Court Building
Manhattan, Kansas 66502

Dear Mr. Ginger:

I am following up our telephone conversation of November 20 to reinforce to you how well my background aligns with the graduate-assistant position you have open for a nontraditional student coordinator.

As a former nontraditional undergraduate here at K-State, I understand the problems and frustrations of those students coming back to school after a delay—especially those who are unable to attend directly on campus. As a lifelong Midwest resident, I am also familiar with the vagaries of the local environment that can affect a person's ability to attend college in a traditional manner.

For these reasons, I am confident that I am eminently qualified for the position as described. I'd like to phone you in the near future to arrange a time to discuss the good ideas I could bring to this position. Thank you very much for your time.

Sincerely,

Jill Berry

Self-Referral Letter

Follow-up of a phone conversation. •————————

He succinctly describes his past accomplishments. •————————

Matthew Pinch
382 E. 22 Street
New York, NY 10020
(212) 555-8928

January 23, 2000

Mr. Paul Johnson
Fashion Interiors, Inc.
32 Beacon Street
Boston, MA 02116

Dear Mr. Johnson:

I very much enjoyed talking with you last Tuesday about your need to fill your firm's architectural and interior-designer position. My seven years of experience as associate-in-charge of the interiors group at a New York architectural firm and as an architectural designer qualify me well for this position.

In my most recent position, I headed up activities ranging from complete coordination and production of construction drawings to furniture inventories, from finish and furniture selections to space planning and design development. I met with clients, identified their needs, and executed their space plans in tenant fit-outs in New York and Philadelphia. As my previous employer can attest, my work was accurate and detail-oriented.

I've been extremely impressed with the fine work Fashion Interiors does, and I'm convinced that I can enhance the firm's success.

Mr. Johnson, I am positive my qualifications are an excellent fit with the position, and it would be mutually beneficial for us to meet. I will call you early next week to set up an appointment for an interview.

Sincerely,

Matthew Pinch

Self-Referral Letter

Follow-up on a previous correspondence. •

The applicant builds on rapport established •
earlier with the recipient.

Skyler Cooper Hathaway
73 Parkwood Drive
Atherton, CA 94027

June 9, 2000

Mr. Brett B. Steele
Snowball.com, Inc.
250 Executive Park Blvd., Ste. 4000
San Francisco, CA 94134

Dear Mr. Steele,

Back in January before I relocated to the Bay Area from Ohio, I wrote to you about the possibility of employment with your dynamic company. You wrote me back an extremely nice letter. You said that with my qualifications, I should have no difficulty finding a job here.

I'm happy to say you were right. I'm working as an online content editor in the marketing department of Sun Microsystems.

Having felt such a nice rapport with you in your very warm letter, I thought you might like to know that I'm here in the Bay Area and am enhancing my ability to make a contribution to a company such as yours.

In addition to the numerous articles and tutorials I've worked at placing on the Sun Web site, I have also been a key member of the site redesign team. I also recently learned that the newsletter I produced in my last job won first place in a regional newsletter competition for nonprofit agencies.

I am still very interested in meeting with you. I'll give you a call in the near future to see if we can set something up. Should you wish to reach me before hearing from me, you may call me at 650-555-2513 during business hours.

Thank you for your consideration, and thanks again for your wonderful letter in January.

Cordially,

Skyler Cooper Hathaway

Self-Referral Letter

Follow-up of a social encounter. •————

Effectively describes how he can fill a need. •————

Gabriel Meenan
187 Salem Road
Tewksbury, MA 01876
(414) 555-2010

May 15, 2000

Ms. Mary Jane Collins
Senator Jack Frost Headquarters
293 Main Street
Boston, MA 02116

Dear Mary Jane,

It was truly delightful to meet you at Senator Frost's brunch on Saturday. Your sense of humor is infectious, and I'm sure it goes a long way in helping you cope with your massive workload.

I'd like to help make your workload and that of your staff lighter. You mentioned at the brunch that the time has come to hire a communications director. I'm convinced I could make a significant contribution in that position.

I have been communications director for the Institute for the Reinvention of Education for two years. I help advance the organization's agenda by developing dynamic campaigns, including one that won an "Award of Distinction" from the Massachusetts Public Relations Association.

Obviously, I am well-versed in cutting-edge education issues. But having worked as a public information director at the Nebraska Association of Social Workers, I am also highly knowledgeable in many other areas in which Senator Frost is taking the lead: infant mortality, prenatal care, teen-pregnancy prevention, and health care.

Mary Jane, I have enclosed some of my favorite campaign materials. I am confident that it would be constructive for us to meet again. I would like to be considered for the communications director position —I'm convinced my qualifications and your needs are a perfect fit.

I'll check in with you at the teacher's union luncheon next week. You may also wish to reach me. During business hours, you can reach me at 555-4800, or leave a message on my home voicemail at 555-2010.

Thanks so much for your consideration. I look forward to talking with you again soon.

Cordially,

Gabriel Meenan

Self-Referral Letter

Recontacting a former employer. •

Note the informal greeting; remember that it's okay only • when you are on a first-name basis with the recipient.

Note the promise to bring story ideas to the interview. •

John A. Pescatello
35 W. Colgate Circle
Great Neck, NY 11021
914-555-2887

August 9, 2000

Mr. Richard McPherson
Executive Editor
Rochester News Leader
Rochester, NY 14610

Dear Dick,

I'm hoping you remember me. I worked for you as a copy editor two years ago, but cut short my employment there to finish my bachelor's degree at Syracuse University. I have just learned that your arts writer is no longer with you. I'm writing to ask you to considering hiring me to replace her.

I have completed degrees in journalism and humanities, which give me the tools that combine journalistic writing and literature, art, and music. For the past year, I've worked in Syracuse University's art gallery as press coordinator, where I've learned and written a great deal about art.

I've written extensively about the arts both during my academic career and while working in the gallery; I've also written lots of other features and have a large portfolio I'd love to share with you. Story ideas are a particular strength; I'll bring twenty story ideas about the arts to our interview if you agree it's worthwhile for us to talk.

I am also very conscious of the strong commitment to the arts by the publisher's family, and I am sure I can do justice to their commitment by setting a high standard of excellence in arts writing at the *News Leader*. I'll also be a cordial representative of the paper to the arts community.

I am sure that you will agree that we should meet again. Knowing that you must be eager to fill the arts-writer position, I'll call to arrange a visit to your office in the next few days. Should you wish to reach me, you may call me during business hours at (914) 555-7506 or at home at (914) 555-2887.

Thank you for your consideration of me. I look forward to meeting with you again.

Cordially,

John A. Pescatello

Self-Referral Letter

Follow-up of career fair.

She invokes professors to add credibility to her self-appraisal.

Sarah Cornett Dinsher
1545 Willowtree Lane, Apt. B5
Ann Arbor, MI 48105
(313) 555-7887
email: sdinsh@umich.edu

October 1, 2000

Ms. Lisa Kessler
J.P. Morgan & Co. Inc.
60 Wall St.
New York, NY 10260

Dear Ms. Kessler,

It was a pleasure to meet you at the Career Fair at the University of Michigan on September 28.

I am a graduate student pursuing my master of science degree in electrical engineering at the University of Michigan; I expect to graduate in December 2000. I am majoring in signal processing and am particularly interested in the position of technology analyst at your organization.

I possess a comprehensive background in statistical signal processing, regression analysis of time-series data, parametric and nonparametric data-modeling techniques, and fairly strong programming skills, as well as the necessary analytical and interpersonal skills required for a challenging position at J.P. Morgan.

While my resume details my qualifications, I also wish to add that I am a quick learner and confident in my ability to meet your expectations in all spheres. My professors can back me up on these points.

If, after reviewing my resume, you agree that I can contribute to your organization's goals, I would appreciate the opportunity to meet you personally. I'll phone you in two weeks to make an appointment. In the meantime, please do not hesitate to contact me by telephone or email.

Thank you for your consideration.

Sincerely,

Sarah Cornett Dinsher

Letter to an Executive-Search Firm

Good use of highlighting. •

Effectively shows how he can increase profitability. •

Dan Bolding
233 K Street
Washington, D.C. 20520
202-555-4812

December 20, 2000

Mr. Sinclair Martin
Honcho-Search.com, Inc.
500 Pennsylvania Avenue
Washington, D.C. 20520

Dear Mr. Martin,

Several associates have mentioned the quality of your search work for managers in this area. Clair Taylor-Jones was particularly complimentary. I think we should get to know one another.

My experience and track record in sales and marketing have been excellent. Here's a brief summary:

- I was promoted to national sales manager after only two years with Art International and effected a 10-percent increase in market share for all products (up to 20 percent for several products). My sales force was revitalized and motivated.
- I increased profitability by reducing costly administrative procedures. By giving the sales people more authority, time-consuming tasks were removed from their agenda, and they were able to do what they do best—sell.
- My track records with all the companies I have been with, from salesman to national sales manager, are all positive—all have shown increased sales.
- My career has been rewarding, but our president has reluctantly agreed with me that to optimize my career possibilities, I should look to a larger organization.

Since I am quite interested in the services you have to offer, I will call you the week of January 8. Feel free to call me at 555-4812 if you wish to speak with me earlier.

Sincerely,

Dan Bolding

Letter to a
Professional Organization

Note how the applicant relates her experience •
to the pharmaceutical industry.

She effectively demonstrates her interest in increasing •
prospective employers' profitability

Hilary Granola
2090 NE Indian Hill Lane
Beaverton, OR 97005
(503) 555-4562

June 30, 2000

Satya Ramidipati
Oregon Biotechnology Association
111 SW Columbia Avenue
Portland, OR 97201

Dear Ms. Ramidipati,

I have learned that your organization is committed to matching the biotech/pharmaceutical openings in member companies with quality applicants. Thus, I am writing to introduce you to a background that should be of great interest to your member firms, and to ask your assistance in my quest for a research position.

My education has been in chemical engineering, while my research training and interests are in molecular and cellular biology.

For the past four years I have been working on my Ph.D. thesis, which concerns secretion of foreign proteins from yeast. I am developing a vector system that allows the gene for a foreign protein to be integrated into the chromosomes of yeast.

This research is directly applicable to the production of pharmaceuticals as well as germane to identifying the key factors of secretion. In the process, I have developed advanced molecular biological lab skills and have been able to apply my engineering expertise to the project.

I am quite flexible on geographic location; I have focused my attention on finding a company where my skills can be fully utilized and a research position where I can make a lasting and profit-making contribution.

If you can be of any assistance in identifying a company that may need a research scientist with my skills and interests, please don't hesitate to pass along a copy of my enclosed resume and extend them an invitation to contact me. In the meantime, I'd like to contact you to brainstorm career strategies with you.

Thank you for your time and assistance.

Sincerely,

Hilary Granola

Letter that Highlights

Cold-contact letter for graduate student. •————

Note the use of bullets to highlight selling points. •————

Demonstrates knowledge of the company. •————

Matthew Pinelas
32 Longleaf Lake Lane
Portland, ME 04105
(207) 555-3832

July 23, 2000

Ms. Stephanie Thomas
Quality Systems Director
Sara Lee Corporation
3 First National Plaza
Chicago, IL 60602-4260

Dear Ms. Thomas,

During my graduate studies, I learned that Sara Lee is a highly respected organization and well-known for its concern for quality and safety. My ability to analyze food systems in terms of equipment, processing, quality, and microbial safety parallels your company's commitment. The value that I can add to your organization, based on more than six years' worth of accomplishments, is summarized below:

- Outstanding written and verbal communication skills that would enable me to write reports and interact with other team members.
- Well-developed analytical and quantitative skills that would allow me to review food systems and processes with precision.
- A unique combination of science and engineering skills developed through course work and research projects.

After you review my qualifications, I would welcome the opportunity to speak with you personally. I will call you during the week of August 7 to ensure that you have received my resume and to answer any questions you might have. If you desire any additional information, I can be reached at (207) 555-3832.

Thank you for considering my qualifications.

Sincerely,

Matthew Pinellas

Letter that Highlights

Date: Tue, 12 Sept 2000 08:26:12
From: Jeffrey P. Chomansky <jeffchom@hotmail.com>
To: hr@webhire.com
Subject: Principal DESIGNER—Interface, ID#: 3204

My ten years of diverse experience in the computer field, including more than four years of design experience with Web-related design projects, make me exactly the kind of value-added employee you need in the position you are advertising.

As a senior Web designer for the Greater Boston Chamber of Commerce and an independent consultant helping clients select, install, and implement Web solutions, my accomplishments and expertise to date include:

— expert knowledge of HTML/graphic design programs
— thorough working knowledge of design-related applications
— determination of cognitive models and development of consistent metaphors, guides, and other information structures underlying particular user interface systems
— creation and design of artistic themes for interface, such as icons, guides, and toolbars
— experience developing, documenting, and implementing various database applications
— implementation of e-commerce packages for consumer and business customers

With my experience, I am positive I can do an outstanding job for your company. Please contact me at my office (617-555-0250) or home (617-555-6346) to arrange a meeting. You can also reach me by email at jeffchom@hotmail.com. Thank you for your consideration.

Sincerely,
Jeffrey P. Chomansky

Jeffrey P. Chomansky
7 Bunker Hill Rd.
Newton, MA 02161

Letter that Highlights

Response to a classified ad.

He does an excellent job of tailoring his experience
to the stated job requirements.

John R. O'Neal
234 Pratt Avenue
Gulfport, MS 39501
(601) 555-1892

September 1, 2000

Ms. Michelle Arnold
Eye World of Gulfport
400 W. Beach Blvd.
Gulfport, MS 39501

Office Manager/Controller
For eyecare facility. Supervisory experience required. Successful candidate
will take responsibility for company budget. Excellent communications
and computer skills needed. Strong skills in finance and accounting a must.
Knowledge of insurance reimbursement systems preferred. Write to:

Ms. Michelle Arnold
Eye World of Gulfport
400 W. Beach Blvd.
Gulfport, MS 39501

Dear Ms. Arnold:

When I read your advertisement for an office manager/controller, I was struck by how closely the requirements of the position align with my experience and skills. Please consider these qualifications in light of
your stated needs:

- I directly supervised a staff of seven professionals; I also indirectly supervised the departmental bud-
gets and expenditures of more than thirty cost-center managers.
- I used my communications skills extensively to brief the executive staff.
- As chief financial officer, I was directly responsible for all financial matters of five departments, and I
was recognized quickly for my skills and abilities.
- I have gained a broad knowledge of accounting from my academic and professional experiences.
- My computer skills are well developed from both managerial and individual-user perspectives.
- I was responsible for the first- and third-party reimbursement program, which was consistently rated
among the best for collection percentages.

I will contact your office within a week regarding an interview. If, on reviewing my credentials in the
meantime, you agree that I am the person you need, please contact me at (601) 555-1892.

Thank you for your time and consideration.

Cordially,

John R. O'Neal

Letter that Highlights

Quantifies her accomplishments effectively. •————

Demonstrates commitment to profitability. •————

Jody Kopetman
85 W. 85th Street
New York, NY 10023
212-555-1960

October 23, 2000

Ms. Carolyn Grant
Manhattan Engineering Supplies
23 Houston Street
New York, NY 10005

Dear Ms. Grant,

In my four years as sales manager of a leading engineering supplies distributor in Long Island, I directed the sales and marketing policies of the company's line of drafting parts and accessories.

During that time:

• Annual billings more than tripled, from $3.25 million to $10.75 million.

• Profits rose five-fold, from $150,000 in 1996 to $785,000 for the fiscal year ending September 2000.

• The number of accounts within the same geographical territory increased by more than 250 percent.

The success I've had here and elsewhere in fifteen years of selling is not a coincidence, or attributable to luck or magic. My sales success results from a natural ability to analyze a marketing/selling situation and come up with an innovative program that leaves the competition way behind.

What I have done for my previous employers, I am confident I can do for you.

Ms. Grant, I will be calling you next week so that we can discuss how I can serve your company in increasing sales and market share. In the meantime, please feel free to contact me at 212-555-1960. Thank you for your time and consideration.

Sincerely yours,

Jody Kopetman

Letter that Highlights

Response to an ad posted on the Internet. •————

He offers supporting evidence for each highlighted item. •————

Dr. Scott Hent
34 Handhewn Way
Manlius, NY 13104
(315) 555-2323
SHent@orange.syracuse.edu

July 28, 2000

Chair of the Search Committee
Department of Plant Biology
State University of New York
Rochester, NY 14610

Dear Search Committee Chair:

The congruity of my scientific research, my teaching, and my program-management experience and your requirements would assure my success in the position of Professor and Chairperson of the Department of Plant Biology that you posted on the BioNET Web site. In particular, the following characteristics and abilities may be of interest to you:

- **Experience in supervising and motivating collaborators.** During my appointment at Syracuse University, I was in charge of planning and conducting courses in plant physiology, anatomy, and evolution.
- **A talent for organizing interdisciplinary teamwork.** At the National Institutes of Health in Bethesda, Maryland, I had the pleasure of cooperating with experts in the areas of phytopathology, virology, immunology, mathematical modeling, image processing, and biomedical engineering. While at Syracuse University, I initiated collaborations with the departments of chemistry, biochemistry, mass spectrometry, and nuclear magnetic resonance.
- **Extensive experience in scientific research.** My latest work concerns macro-molecular analysis and the development of innovative tools for characterizing intact viruses, cell organelles, and large DNA molecules using nondenaturing techniques.

I offer an enthusiastic approach, a consistent work ethic, and diverse experience in all aspects of program management and interdisciplinary scientific research, as any of my colleagues can verify. One of my goals would be to provide academic and administrative leadership to promote excellence in teaching and research in the Department of Plant Physiology.

Thank you for your consideration. I look forward to the opportunity to explain in greater detail how I can be effective in this position. Should you have any questions, you may call me at (315) 555-2323.

Sincerely,

Scott Hent, Ph.D.

Clever Angle Letter

Note the effective transition from clever opening paragraph to serious second paragraph.

This applicant relates her broad experience and interests to the job specifics.

Sara Dent Bernier
3256 N. A1A, #34
Vero Beach, FL 32963
(561) 555-8118

February 22, 2000

Mr. Doug Jackson
Sci-Fi Channel
USA Networks, Inc.
152 W. 52nd St.
New York, NY 10019

Dear Mr. Jackson:

You are about to enter a dimension as vast as space and as timeless as infinity. It is the middle ground between light and shadow, between science and superstition. It lies between the pit of man's fears and the summit of his knowledge. This is the dimension of imagination. It is an area we call...The Sci-Fi Channel.

To bridge the gap between humankind's fears and the summit of human knowledge, you will need competent legal counsel who understands both the cable arena and science fiction. I am applying to be that counsel to The Sci-Fi Channel.

I can bring to this position not only quality legal counsel, but a passion for science fiction, extraordinary research experience, and even a broadcasting background that ranges from *Jeopardy!* contestant to finalist in the network management division of the Academy of Television Arts and Sciences Program.

I will graduate from Stetson University College of Law in April and take the Florida Bar exam in July. My degree emphasizes corporate and media law. My legal work experience has focused on governmental law, and I am experienced in dealing with all varieties of bureaucrats.

Through my undergraduate major in communications, with an emphasis in film, media, public relations, and journalism, I have developed a keen understanding of all aspects of the television broadcasting industry, as well as the ability to communicate effectively to all types and groups of people.

I'd like to telephone you before visiting your area in April to pinpoint a time when we could meet to discuss the excellent fit between my background and your needs. Thanks so much for your time and attention.

Best wishes,

Sara Dent Bernier

Clever Angle Letter

April J. Jacobs
13 Winding Winds Way
Atlanta, GA 30308
(404) 555-9528

March 8, 2000

Mr. Samuel L. Lopez
VP, Public Relations
Georgia-Pacific Corporation
Georgia-Pacific Center
133 Peachtree St. NE
Atlanta, GA 30303

Dear Mr. Lopez,

In my last two editing positions, a thirty-gallon trash can in my office has been the destination of 90 percent of the press releases I received. I could write a book or teach a course on how not to write a news release or mount a publicity campaign.

I know what editors are looking for. I know because for the past year and a half, I was executive editor of a group of ten weekly newspapers in the Atlanta area. Before that, I was city editor for the newspaper in Georgia's third-largest city. I'm now managing editor of a new consumer magazine that, unfortunately, is relocating to California soon.

My inside track on the media would be enormously useful in running your public relations department. I have good contacts in the press, and know how to approach the media. I also have the ability to handle breaking news of the sort that presents great challenges to Fortune 500 companies such as Georgia-Pacific.

Finally, I have considerable successful management experience, having supervised as many as thirty reporters and editors simultaneously. I also possess the exceptional organizational skills needed to create media plans.

I'd like to set up an interview at your convenience and will call you at the beginning of the month to schedule it. You may also reach me during business hours at 404-555-2660 or leave a message at 404-555-9528.

Thanking you most kindly for your consideration of me. I look forward to meeting with you soon.

Cordially,

April J. Jacobs

Clever Angle Letter

Uses referral technique. •————

Uses humor to make a point. •————

Effective approach for a career changer; •————
turns a "no" into a "yes."

Sheri Kelling
1251 H Street 34
Bellingham, WA 98225
Phone: 206-555-9733

February 14, 2000

Mr. Jim R. Bradley
Human Resources
Microsoft Corporation
1 Microsoft Way
Redmond, WA 98052-6399

Dear Mr. Bradley:

Dr. Burbank N. Rayos suggested that I write to you regarding the position of Senior Human Resources Assistant and its requirement for someone who can maintain a steady course despite many interruptions.

Let's talk about interruptions. Whoops, there's the phone. Excuse me . . . Now I have new email. Sorry about that—now where was I? Oh yes, I was explaining that interruptions aren't a problem. I can keep many complex projects going at once and haven't yet pulled out all my hair.

I'm assuming by "self-starter" you mean someone who finds out the criteria for the desired outcome and simply goes and does it, checking in whenever it's appropriate. That's how I like to work—and I've done it well, according to my supervisors.

I am a grown-up. I like to take on responsibility. I learn very quickly, I have a good attitude, and I thrive on making my boss successful.

Now here's the thing. My experience is not actually in human resources, but here's what I can offer: a master's degree in organization development with a lot of related study in human resources, such as employee enrichment, meeting-design and facilitation, training and development, and a little continuous quality improvement thrown in for good measure. I decided to switch careers, so I went back to graduate school, and human resources is where I want to be. I am confident you'll find that my experience, plus my general smarts and whole-systems approach, will be valuable to your organization.

I look forward to the opportunity of meeting with you and will call you next week to make an appointment.

Sincerely,

Sheri Kelling

Clever Angle Letter

The opening paragraph is a grabber. •

Response to a classified ad. •

Jay Bayne
101 Church Street
Mobile, AL 36608
(334) 555-2124

October 24, 2000

Dr. Amy Barrett
University of Central Florida
Department of Biology
Orlando, FL 32816

Dear Dr. Barrett:

You would not know that I am an avid fisherman from reading my resume. But then neither would you realize that I am adaptable, aggressively intellectual, cooperative, goal-oriented, and a team player. I take great pleasure in the theories and practices of science and in the possibility of contributing to an ever-growing pool of knowledge.

I am applying for the Biologist Assistant position because I enjoy field biology and have a deep interest in conservation. My past experiences have involved extensive radiotelemetry work on a variety of species. I have independently tracked 30+ raccoons, studied radio-tagged Mexican spotted owls in southern Utah, and aided in the release of three tagged peregrine falcons. I am familiar with a variety of telemetry equipment, as well as the analysis of telemetry data.

Coupled with my extensive telemetry work is a thorough knowledge of orienteering, including the use of compasses and GPSs. My graduate work provided bountiful opportunities to practice and refine my technical writing skills, including the preparation of a thesis and biannual reports of my progress to the funding agency.

I am excited about the position, and I would appreciate the opportunity to work for you. My former employers can attest that if you hire me you will be getting a sincere, hard-working wildlife biologist.

Now that I've introduced myself, I hope you'll take the opportunity to get to know me better through an interview. I would enjoy talking to you on the phone or visiting the area to learn more about UCF and the position, so I'll call you next week to see if we can pinpoint a time to meet.

Sincerely,

Jay Bayne

Cold-Contact Letter

Quantifies accomplishments in the opening paragraph. •————

Jan P. Wood
4354 Winter Ave. W.
Los Angeles, CA 98765
(562) 555-8832

She makes effective use of her Unique Selling •————
Proposition in the third paragraph.

October 10, 2000

Mr. Kirk Horton
Human Resources Manager
Fantastic Software
P.O. Box 1434
Mountain View, CA 94045-1434

Dear Mr. Horton:

Are you seeking an experienced product marketing professional? Could you use a marketer whose efforts contributed to a flagship product's 800-percent increase in sales revenues over three years? I am that marketer.

As the Director of Marketing at Pegboard Press Publishing, I enjoyed the opportunity to be involved in every aspect of marketing, from strategic planning to package design to managing successful product launches. My contributions to Pegboard resulted in its flagship product, *Hearth and Home Cookbook,* achieving and maintaining the top position in its category.

I am confident that my consumer software marketing experience, and my ability to successfully manage budgets, schedules, and project teams would enable me to contribute significantly to Fantastic Software. My outstanding analytical and communication skills, strong customer focus, creativity, and enthusiasm would be valuable assets as well.

Should an appropriate position become available, I would greatly appreciate the opportunity to discuss my qualifications with you. I'll phone you during the next quarter to check on openings. You may also reach me at (562) 555-8832. Thank you very much for your consideration and I look forward to meeting with you.

Sincerely,

Jan P. Wood

Cold-Contact Letter

Sums up her accomplishments nicely in a few paragraphs. •

Note the strong third paragraph. •

Gretchen Speck
1050 W. 100th Circle
Westminster, CO 80021
(303) 555-5683

September 18, 2000

Isabel Hughes, Program Director
WDYZ
100 Rocky Mountain Road
Denver, CO 80230

Dear Ms. Hughes,

Because I have developed and produced an informative celebrity-interview show and have done Air Talent shifts at several radio stations, I am confident that I have the qualities to serve in an Air Talent/Talk Show Host capacity at your station.

Talkfest, the show I oversaw from its inception to its current success, featured interviews with such celebrities as radio personality Don Imus, actors Tom Hanks and Cybill Shepherd, talk-show host Montel Williams, U.S. Senator Ted Kennedy of Massachusetts, and many others. I've enclosed a tape of *Talkfest* highlights.

Former station managers can tell you that I'm organized, dependable, and capable of handling multiple tasks. I'm not only a talented announcer, but am deft at production, able to write copy, news, and sports, and can manage front-desk duties.

I am convinced that it would be mutually fruitful for us to discuss how I can contribute to your station's ongoing success. I will contact you next week to set up a meeting. If you'd like to reach me before that, please call (303) 555-5683.

Thanks so much, Ms. Hughes, for considering me.

Sincerely,

Gretchen Speck

Cold-Contact Letter

Effectively presents the applicant's •
Unique Selling Proposition.

Packs solid information into just a few paragraphs. •

Sammy Pietro
29 Hillsdale Drive
Battle Creek, MI
(616) 555-1336

September 13, 2000

Ms. Mariah Fisch, President
National Steel Corporation
4100 Edison Lakes Pkwy.
Mishawaka, IN 46545-3440

Dear Ms. Fisch,

During eighteen years of manufacturing experience, most of it in project management, I've made it a priority to continually develop my business skill set with an eye toward emerging trends. My use of Enterprise Resource Planning (ERP) software, most recently using SAP (but with exposure to ERPs from PeopleSoft and Oracle), has provided me with the opportunity to gain wide experience in manufacturing systems, demonstrate my ability to successfully lead projects, and develop the discipline required to perform while standing at the center of the storm.

I'd like to bring those skills to your company. I will fulfill my personal goal of ten years with Harris Semiconductor in October. I would be very interested in talking with you about opportunities at National Steel.

As the Harris Semiconductor project leader charged with the implementation of our scheduling system utilizing SAP, I reported directly to the plant manager and took charge of weekly progress presentations to the VP/GM and his staff. The project touched every corner of our business and my implementation teams came from every major functional discipline. I'm proud to say that the scheduling system is now the backbone of our factory system integration.

I'd like to meet with you to see if I can do for you what I did for Harris. I'll contact you in two weeks to arrange a meeting.

Regards,

Sammy Pietro

Cold-Contact Letter

Krystan V. Siesnen
283 E. Central Avenue
Moorestown, NJ 08507
856-555-5665

September 14, 2000

Mr. Stephen Tate
Tate, Kief & Philips Advertising
100 University Blvd., 15th Floor
Princeton, NJ 08540

Dear Mr. Tate,

As advertising agencies are increasingly being evaluated on the development of advertising campaigns that guarantee success, there is a growing need for trained and experienced professionals in the field.

Through my years of advertising experience and my master's degree in integrated marketing communications, I am certain I could give you valuable assistance in satisfying client demands for top-quality work, while also providing strong leadership skills.

I will complete my master's degree in December and would be interested in making a contribution to Tate, Kief & Philips Advertising's profitability in a client-services capacity.

I am positive my experience and talents would be useful to you, and I will call you in late September to discuss an interview.

Thank you for your time and consideration. I look forward to speaking with you.

Sincerely,

Krystan V. Siesnen

Cold-Contact Letter

The opener grabs attention. ●————

He quantifies his past success. ●————

He makes a strong case for the skills and ●———— accomplishments he would bring to the job.

Daniel Swanson
232 Mountain Drive
Denver, CO 80210
303-555-2332

June 23, 2000

Ms. Samantha Montgomery
First Colorado Insurance Co.
75 Mountain Lakes Drive
Denver, CO 80210

Dear Ms. Montgomery,

According to the local newspaper, there were more than 200 "suspicious" fires in Denver in 1999. Of those 200+ fires, only about 20 were ever officially logged as arson. That's less than a 10-percent success ratio.

My 15 years as a fire marshall with the Denver Fire Department and my seven years as fire investigator with Rocky Mountain Insurance Company, Inc.—where my arson success ratio is close to 50 percent—qualify me for the position of Chief Fire Investigator.

My work with the arson squad of the Denver Fire Department earned high praise and three citations from the mayor's office. My work with Rocky Mountain has saved the company millions of dollars in fraudulent fire claims.

Although I am happy in my present job, and Rocky Mountain is certainly more than satisfied with my work, I feel it's time to move from being a player to becoming a manager, where, with my keen sense for investigation. I can lead a team and help your company save millions of dollars.

I would like to discuss my qualifications more fully with you in the near future. I will call you next Tuesday to see if we can find an agreeable time.

Thank you for your time and consideration.

Sincerely,

Daniel Swanson

Cold-Contact Letter

Roscoe D. Reynolds
PO Box 231
Tellico Plains, TN 37385
423-555-2358
mrmarketing@aol.com

October 8, 2000

Mr. Judson Beasley
VP, Marketing & Distribution
Coca-Cola, Inc.
1 Coca-Cola Plaza
Atlanta, GA 30313

Dear Mr. Beasley,

I am a seasoned professional and a highly successful and competent team member with a background of extensive "hands on" experience in manufacturing, service, and distribution market segments. My success has been both inward to the operating unit level and outward to the financial and supplier entities. I'd like to bring that success to your company in a marketing distribution capacity.

As a profit-oriented manager with a proven track record and a bias toward responsible growth and effective utilization of costs and overhead, I bring an absolutely positive "can do!" attitude to the work place. "But we have never done it that way" is NOT an operational part of my vocabulary.

I am well versed in the applicable concepts and implementation of managerial and fiscal reporting necessary for a successful business enterprise. I have experience with various text and word processing applications; computer packages, such as SAS, SPSS, and MiniTab; applications such as VALS, MAPICS, SOTAS, ACCPAC, and BAS, as well as industry-specific packages. I have been extremely successful in accounting system conversions between heterogeneous systems, and have some exposure to ERPs.

Relocation is not an impediment. I am willing to travel extensively.

I am positive it would be worthwhile for us to meet. I will contact you in a week to arrange a meeting. Should you have any questions before that time, please feel free to reach me by phone at 423-555-2358, or by email at mrmarketing@aol.com.

Very truly yours,

Roscoe D. Reynolds

Cold-Contact Letter

Ross Pesmen
103 Top Line Drive, Apt. 32
Milwaukee, Wisconsin 53202
Tel: (414) 555-3471
Fax: (414) 555-1003

July 15, 2000

Ms. Carol Seachrist
MascoTech, Inc.
21001 Van Born Rd.
Taylor, MI 48180

Dear Ms. Seachrist:

My solid experience in project leadership, full life-cycle development of sales-force automation systems, trouble-shooting, and customer support, combined with my background in client-server and relational databases, would enable me to enhance your success in software development at MascoTech, Inc. Both my master's and bachelor's degrees are in computer science, with a minor in accounting.

As any of my former employers can attest, I am a self-motivated, hands-on, results-oriented software developer who continuously demonstrates a high level of commitment and a strong work ethic. I am also a strong team player who will exert every effort to ensure that the goals of the team are met.

Thanks to my technical background, as well as my clear understanding of the customer's business process, I am recognized as a valuable resource for providing input and ideas. My excellent communication skills and accurate verbal content allow me to effectively communicate with people at all levels.

This combination of skills gives me a solid foundation upon which to make an immediate and meaningful contribution to your establishment. If upon reviewing my qualifications you agree that I would be able to contribute to the plans and goals of MascoTech, I would be pleased to meet with you to further discuss my background. I will contact you the week of July 31 to arrange a meeting. Should you have any questions before that time, you may reach me at (414) 555-3471 or by email at pesmen@highlife.wisconsin.edu.

Thank you for your time and consideration.

Sincerely,

Ross Pesmen

Letter Seeking
Consulting/Freelance Work

The opener is a grabber. •————

He targets a very specific niche in his field. •————

Jeff H. Lucas
262 Buckhead Lane
Atlanta, GA 30026
(404) 555-3292
Email: jhlucas@earthlink.net

February 2, 2000

Mr. Dabney Greer
Director of Marketing
National Service Industries, Inc.
1420 Peachtree St., NE
Atlanta, GA 30309-3002

Dear Mr. Greer:

As you know, it's the hottest companies that need extra resources during crunch times, so you might want to keep my card close at hand.

I recently relocated to Atlanta from San Francisco, where I worked as the information designer in Macromedia, Inc.'s online publishing tools department (which accounts for 83 percent of sales). There, I wrote the company's marketing collateral—from product data sheets, Web pages, and packaging and position papers to videoscripts and multimedia applications.

I have a strong background in marketing and public relations, great product-management skills, wide exposure to Web-authoring and development software, and a good working knowledge of the most popular graphics and multimedia-authoring software.

My broad range of skills makes it easy for me to jump in and get the job done. Whether you need new marketing collateral for your company or a new product, a story pitched to the media, assistance in planning for an upcoming trade show, or extra help in finishing a multimedia production or Web design—my skills may be just what you need.

So do keep me in mind during your next crunch period. I'd be happy to send you samples of my work and talk with you about how my skills and experience could be strong assets for National Service Industries, Inc. I'll call you to touch base after the Multimedia convention; maybe I'll even see you there.

Sincerely,

Jeff H. Lucas

Classified Ad Response Letter

Succinctly describes how her experience •
relates to job requirements.

Kimberly Long
372 Main Street
Los Altos, CA 94022
(310) 555-3334

October 15, 2000

Ms. JoAnn Greenfield
Planned Parenthood, Inc.
P.O. Box 383
Mountain View, CA 94045

Dear Ms. Greenfield:

My degree in nutrition and my work with the Women, Infants, and Children supplemental food program align nicely with your needs in the research-assistant position you are currently advertising.

My work with the American Heart Association, which focused on the prevention of coronary heart disease through a healthy lifestyle, would be extremely helpful in developing a clearinghouse of wellness/health promotion.

I could also bring legislative-staff and task-force experience to the wellness/health program, as I have a thorough understanding of the operations of California government.

Ms. Greenfield, I am confident that my qualifications are an excellent fit with this position and that it would be expedient for us to meet. I will give you a call early next week to set up an interview.

Thank you for your consideration.

Sincerely,

Kimberly Long

Classified Ad Response Letter

Note the attention-getting opening paragraph. •

Phil Caldwell
327 Handy Way
Normal, IL 61761
(309) 555-2234

May 30, 2000

Dr. Mavis Fennelly
Department of Engineering
Illinois State University
Normal, IL 61760

Dear Dr. Fennelly,

Would you like your Engineering Center Manager to be someone who has conducted extensive research on the major obstacles to successful careers in engineering? Someone who has a solid applied background as an award-winning mechanical engineer? Someone with the experience and pedagogical ideas needed to teach engineering skills effectively? Someone with advanced proficiency with computers and CAD? I have the experience and vision that would enable me to make a real difference to the Engineering Center.

I am currently researching and developing a career guide for college engineering students. One aspect of this research has been to survey college faculty members nationwide on the major issues that engineering students encounter. As a result of this research, I have a solid understanding of the major problem areas, and I have developed techniques for targeting the barriers to successful careers in engineering.

As you require, I am completely adept on the Macintosh. In addition to using Macintosh systems in my job for the last several years, I've had my own Mac system at home for more than seven years. My knowledge of PCs includes a thorough understanding of the UNIX and Windows environments, and my ability to use PCs is superior.

I have tutored dozens of students in engineering skills and have developed syllabi for engineering courses. I am thoroughly committed to helping college students develop engineering skills to become successful not only as students, but in their careers—and in life.

Dr. Fennelly, I am eager to meet with you. I'll call you at the beginning of next week to arrange a mutually convenient time. Should you wish to reach me, you may call me at home at (309) 555-2234 or at work at (309) 555-5500.

Thanks so much for your interest and attention.

Cordially,

Phil Caldwell

Classified Ad Response Letter

Cynthia Davis
328 W. Joyce Kilmer Court
Salt Lake City, UT 84106
(801) 555-4343

March 16, 2000

Mr. Sam N. David
Movies Unlimited
100 Main Street
Salt Lake City, UT 84105

Dear Mr. David,

Congratulations on the opening of your new store. Your ad leads me to believe you and I share a philosophy about customer service. That's why I'm eager to bring my experience in working with the public—combined with a love of movies and a near-photographic memory that enables me to quickly learn stock—to the customer-service representative position you are advertising for the new eastside Movies Unlimited store.

Building on my retail experience from several years ago, I have a steady and reliable work history of positions that would make me an excellent worker for your store.

I am a mature college student at BYU. I have just a very few credit-hours to finish up this summer and fall to obtain my degree, and I could easily work those few classes around a full and flexible schedule at Movies Unlimited. I am perfectly willing to work evenings, weekends, and holidays.

I am truly convinced Movies Unlimited and I are an excellent fit. What's really important to me is to contribute to your bottom line while working with interesting people and movies—close to home.

I'm intelligent, and any of my references and previous employers can tell you that I am a hard worker. Mr. David, I hope you'll give me a chance to show you how I can enhance your new operation. Shall we meet soon so you can learn more about my skills? I'll call you next week to make an appointment.

Thanks very much.

Cordially,

Cynthia Davis

Classified Ad Response Letter

Robert Z. Flick
1861 E. 39th Street
Brooklyn, NY 11229
(718) 555-3264

July 3, 2000

Mr. Sean Jackson
National Broadcasting Company, Inc.
30 Rockefeller Plaza
New York, NY 10112

Dear Mr. Jackson:

A work history can tell you only the bare bones of my story. You can get that from the enclosed resume. This letter is to help you get to know me and show you why I would make a great producer.

I am a broadcaster, experienced in the radio and television fields. Though I've worked for several radio and television affiliates in my career, I've determined that I can make the biggest difference at the network level. I'd like to make that difference for your network in the producer job you are advertising.

Hands on! That's how I learned and how I work. My goal is to become indispensable to a station. When given the opportunity to bring my enthusiasm to your workplace, I can show you the difference between being just an employee and being a driven, goal-oriented team player. That is exactly what I did in my last job at the NBC affiliate in Albany, WALY.

Within a few days of your receiving this letter, I'll call on you personally to arrange a face-to-face meeting. I am looking forward to meeting you and bringing my talents to the network.

Sincerely,

Robert Z. Flick

Classified Ad Response Letter

Debra Nicholson Burbank
3283 Longhorn Drive
Austin, TX 78712
(512) 555-2821

May 15, 2000

Mr. James Jenkins, Training Manager
Department of Human Resources
United Way of New Mexico
12800 Indian School Rd.
Albuquerque, NM 87112

Dear Mr. Jenkins,

My experience as a teacher and writer qualifies me to fill the position you advertised in the May 14 edition of the *Albuquerque Journal* for independent contractors to teach business English.

I have had extensive experience teaching writing at various levels, from Remedial Writing to Advanced Expository Prose and Creative Writing–Prose Fiction, at the University of New Mexico and the University of Albuquerque; additionally, I have taught traditional grammar.

As a university instructor at the University of Texas and elsewhere, I have taught adults exclusively. I have received excellent evaluations from my students, especially those in Advanced Expository Prose. When my regular sections filled to capacity, students have asked me to offer independent studies courses in writing and research.

As a professional technical writer, both as an independent contractor and with a local firm, Strategic Communication, Inc., I am qualified to teach technical writing.

I think you'll agree that a meeting would be both appropriate and mutually beneficial. Please allow me to call you within the next few weeks to arrange an appointment.

Thank you very much for your consideration.

Sincerely,

Debra Nicholson Burbank

Classified Ad Response Letter

R. Thomas Burlington
302 Bentley Circle
Champaign, IL 61820
312-555-5342

April 10, 2000

Mr. Kevin O'Horn
The Quaker Oats Company
Quaker Tower
321 N. Clark St.
Chicago, IL 60610-4714

Dear Mr. O'Horn,

Because I've recently completed a major overhaul of Star Cookies at General Foods Corp., your display ad in last Sunday's *Tribune* for a Brand Manager at Quaker Oats is of special interest to me since it calls for qualifications that completely correspond to my background.

As you can see on my resume, in addition to an excellent professional background in brand management, I have had particular success with new product introductions, twice being promoted because of my ideas and innovations.

While my successes have come often, I have gone as far as I can with General Foods and am ready to take on new challenges at Quaker Oats. I have had ten solid years of brand management experience and now want to bring my ideas and knowledge to your firm.

May I ask you to read my resume and then allow me to phone your secretary next week for an appointment? In the interim, please feel free to call me at 312-555-5342. I look forward to meeting you and thank you for your time and consideration.

Sincerely,

R. Thomas Burlington

Classified Ad Response Letter

Abigail Doyle
101 Franklin Blvd.
Summit, NJ 07901
908-555-1010

August 20, 2000

Ms. Juliet Romanio
James Sharpe Elementary School
4567 Springfield Avenue
Newark, NJ 07103

Dear Ms. Romanio,

Perhaps I am the "multi-talented teacher" you seek in your "Multi-Talented Teacher" advertisement in today's *Newark Star-Ledger*. I'm a versatile teacher, ready to substitute, if necessary, as early as next week. I have the solid teaching experience you specify.

As you will note on the enclosed resume, I am presently affiliated with a highly regarded private elementary school. Mr. Russell, the headmaster, will certainly give you a good reference.

The details of your advertisement suggest to me that the position will involve many of the same responsibilities that I am currently performing.

In addition to the planning, administrating, and student-parent counseling activities I highlight in my resume, please note that I have a master's degree as well as a teaching certificate from the state of New Jersey.

Knowing how frantic you must be without a fifth-grade teacher this close to the beginning of the school year, I will call you in a few days. Or if, upon reviewing my letter and resume, you agree that I am the teacher you need, call me at the home number listed above or at 908-555-3060 during business hours.

Thanking you most sincerely for your time and consideration.

Cordially,

Abigail Doyle

Classified Ad Response Letter

Extremely effective format for tailoring experience to requirements of the job.

Note the particularly assertive closing.

Patty Hathaway
17 Elm Court
Stamford, CT 06902
(475) 555-1732

January 5, 2000

Mr. Edward Ferrara
Human Resources Director
Xerox Corporation
800 Long Ridge Rd.
Stamford, CT 06904

Dear Mr. Ferrara,

 Your advertisement in today's *Wall Street Journal* stimulated my interest and seems to match exactly my particular background and skills.

You Require:	My Qualifications:
Advanced degree	I have an MBA from the Wharton School, specializing in accounting.
10 years accounting experience	4 years, Accountant at Philip Morris in large corporate environment; 3 years, Senior Accountant at AT&T; 4 years, Accounts, PriceWaterhouseCoopers.
Manager of EDP applications	Designed integrated EDP invoicing system for AT&T. IBM, Digital, mainframe experience.

 Since my experience and knowledge fit your requirements exactly, I am clearly one of the people you'll want to see. I plan to call you the week of January 10 to see about setting up an interview. In the meantime, please feel free to call me at my home number as listed above. I look forward to our meeting.
 Thank you for your time and consideration.

Sincerely,

Patty Hathaway

Classified Ad Response Letter

Good example of military transition.

Resulted in an interview followed by a job offer.

Chad Lee Forte
480 Cotton Bay Drive, #44
West Palm Beach, FL 33406
(561) 555-1134

March 29, 2000

Mr. Marc Miller
Miller, Cohen & Company
1300 S. Olive Avenue
West Palm Beach, FL 33406

Dear Mr. Miller,

I was very pleased to see your advertisement for an accountant that recently appeared in the *Miami Herald* because the position is well suited to both my professional and educational background.

The direct responsibilities of my position in the United States Navy closely parallel the requirements of your advertised position. It was solely my responsibility to manage, track, and report the financial position of the hospital, which included accounting for income-statement and balance-sheet items. I also gained valuable experience in preparing short- to intermediate-length (quarterly to annual) term budgets for the medical facility, which consisted of more than thirty specialized departments.

In addition to my experience in the Navy, I have enjoyed numerous other accounting positions outside of the health-care field; I have another seven years' experience in both the restaurant and retail industries, during which I performed general-ledger accounting bank reconciliations, financial statement preparation, and most other accounting functions.

My wife and I have recently moved to West Palm Beach, where she has begun a tenure-track faculty position in the School of Business Administration at Florida Atlantic University. Mr. Miller, knowing how pressed you must be to fill this position, I will contact your office within a week regarding an interview. If, on reviewing my credentials in the meantime, you agree that I am the person you need, please contact me at the home number listed above.

Cordially,

Chad Lee Forte

Classified Ad Response Letter

Keith M. Edmunds
393 Peach Tree Drive, #7
Naperville, IL 60042.
(630) 555-2390

September 19, 2000

Ms. S. A. Ying
Becton Dickinson & Co.
505 State Street
Des Plaines, IL 60016

Dear Ms. Ying,

The ad for a mechanical engineer position in the Sept. 10 *National Ad Search* leads me to believe you seek a person with my ability to handle multiple tasks while meeting high efficiency standards and reducing costs.

With both a bachelor's and master's degree in mechanical engineering, I am well qualified for the position described. I have a strong technical background in design and analysis. In my position as a materials engineer for a medical-electronics company, I am accustomed to working in a fast-paced environment.

I seek a challenging position that provides the opportunity to work hard to help the company attain its goals.

I look forward to talking with you so that I can share with you my background and enthusiasm for the job. I will contact you in ten days to arrange a meeting. Should you wish to reach me in the meantime, please feel free to call me at (630) 555-2390. If I am not in, please leave a message and I will return your call within a day.

Thank you for your time and consideration.

Sincerely,

Keith M. Edmunds

Blind-Box Ad Response Letter

Succinctly describes accomplishments. •

Resulted in an interview. •

Monique Anne Bleuel
128 Watergate Blvd., #34
Washington, D.C. 20015
(202) 555-0766

July 17, 2000

Box 435
Washington Post
Washington, D.C. 20009

Dear Boxholder:

My work as both the Chief Financial Officer and Chief of Computer Systems Management at the
Washington Qwik-Care provides me with a solid background to contribute to the success of your firm in
the COO/Medical Data Processing Director position advertised in the *Post*.

As Chief Financial Officer, I was responsible for all first- and third-party billings for medical services
rendered. In times of rising health care costs, my department made aggressive efforts to collect funds due
to the center; successful collections could then be incorporated into the operating budget.

As Chief of Computer Systems Management, I oversaw every aspect of computer operations within
the center—from large projects, such as bringing entirely new networks online, to smaller tasks, such as
performing system backups.

After reviewing my credentials, I am sure you will agree that I am the person you need. Please contact
me at the home number listed above so that we can arrange an interview.

Cordially,

Monique Anne Bleuel

Blind-Box Ad Response Letter

Linda Smith-Davis
2053 Dogwood Lane
Oakland, CA 94620
510-555-9219

August 23, 2000

Dear Boxholder,

Certain key words in your ad lead me to believe I may well be the perfect candidate for this retail management opening, and I'm ready to make a real contribution.

Organizing is a magic word to me because it's what I do best. Virtually all my previous positions have required a detail-oriented and successful organizer to pull everything together. Nowhere has this been more true than in my current position as a production manager in San Francisco's largest ad agency.

Retail environment evokes satisfying memories of the work I did in my last position as men's apparel buyer for Macy's. I thrive in the fast pace and exciting atmosphere of retailing, as Dawn Bachman attests in her letter of recommendation, enclosed per your request.

Advertising and publicity are magic words because I have lots to contribute in these two areas. My previous positions have always involved me in promotional strategy, especially as sales manager for Beaumont Leather Goods, Inc. Combined with my academic experience in advertising and marketing, I have a well-rounded portfolio of skills to add to your sales and profits.

Career opportunity is perhaps the most magic phrase of all, as I have long been searching for a job that I could fully develop long-term. This one seems so perfect because it combines my interest and experience in retail with my organizational talents and promotions expertise.

I would be most happy to make myself available for an interview at your convenience. Thanking you for your consideration, I look forward to hearing from you in the very near future.

Sincerely,

Linda Smith-Davis

Blind-Box Ad Response Letter

The opening paragraph is a grabber because the applicant seems to offer such a good "fit."

Fred N. Sarkisian
23 Library Lane
Plainview, NY 11803
(516) 555-2921

September 14, 2000

UU245
New York Times
Times, NY 10018

Dear Boxholder:

As I read your ad in the *New York Times* for a research manager for a top consumer magazine, I knew immediately that I could offer exactly the solid marketing-research experience and analytical skills you describe.

In my current position as a marketing analyst for a leading market-research firm, I have projected future growth of various industries by researching and analyzing past performance. My analytical skills have contributed to my ability to solve and prevent problems both in my current position and in a previous position with a list broker.

I could bring to your marketing-research position the finely honed communications skills that would enable me to translate research data into readable language. I currently write press releases and direct-mail marketing brochures.

My college thesis, "Developing Cost-Effective Advertising Campaigns," demonstrates my thorough understanding of magazine advertising and other media that compete for advertising dollars.

I also possess considerable supervisory skills, having successfully motivated subordinates and coordinated their activities.

I am confident that my qualifications and your needs are an excellent fit, and it would be in both our best interests to meet. I can make myself available for an appointment at your earliest convenience. Please feel free to call me at (516) 555-2921.

Sincerely,

Fred N. Sarkisian

Blind-Box Ad Response Letter

The second paragraph effectively describes a philosophy • that the recipient may find appealing.

Tiffany Kamber
400 Carter Street
Chattanooga, TN 37402
(423) 555-0218

December 10, 2000

Managing Partner
P.O. Box 5555
Chattanooga, TN 37410-5555

Dear Managing Partner:

I note that your needs for the Executive Secretary/Administrative Assistant position you are currently advertising coincide with my skills and experience. Your ad particularly details the core requirements of my position at Cravens, Smythe, and Harrison, P.A., a management function at which I enjoyed great success.

The environment of the law firm at which I worked was composed of diverse professionals. What I found to be most productive for the operation was developing cooperative working relationships with the staff. In this setting, a judicious mixture of solid interpersonal skills, adaptability to others' needs, and a sincere demeanor was needed. I worked hard to emphasize these traits to my staff, and we built an efficient and cohesive team that was recognized as highly competent and customer service-oriented.

My department administered the financial/accounting and information-system needs for the entire facility. The law firm utilized information-system networks for various functions, including accounts payable, billings, and productivity accounting.

Should you wish to reach me for an interview, you may call or leave a message at (423) 555-0218. Although I will be out of the area from the 16th through the 31st to spend the holidays with my family, I plan to review my phone messages frequently. In addition, I will be available for work immediately after my return. I look forward to talking with you.

Sincerely,

Tiffany Kamber

Effectively relates experience to job requirements. •——————————

Shows strong understanding of the organization's needs. •——————————

Date: Tue, 3 Apr 2000 09:17:48
From: Lisa Anne Knauth <lisaaknauth@hotmail.com>
To: James Griffin jgriffin@corp.disney.com
Subject: Legal activitist ready to tackle DIS-35

Dear Mr. Griffin,

As you and your team prepare to bring the international 2000 Women's Softball Jubilee to the Disney Sports Complex, you will be seeking people with good organization and networking skills. I am one of those people. In response to your ad on the Disney Careers Web site (DIS-35), I am interested in augmenting the team's operation in a legal or management capacity.

My legal experience has been mainly in government and environmental law, while my academic background has been primarily in international law and communications, with an emphasis on broadcasting and public relations.

During a diverse career as an archivist, law clerk, and workshop instructor, I have developed organization and networking skills, a talent for efficiently gathering information from government officials and written sources, and the ability to work well with clients on various projects. I also speak and write fluent French, German, and Spanish.

I will contact you at the end of the month to arrange a convenient interview time. Should you wish to contact me, please do so via email. Thank you for your consideration.

Regards,
Lisa Anne Knauth

Shows understanding of the PEP formula. •————————————

Date: Mon, 9 Oct 2000 12:25:21
From: Elise Bentley White <ebwhite@aol.com>
To: hcadmin@broadmead.org
Subject: Experienced nurse for Director of Nursing position

Dear Health Care Administrator,

My knack for interacting with people, coupled with more than five years of nursing experience, make me an ideal candidate for the director of nursing position you advertised on the MiracleWorkers.com Web site.

In my present position with Inner Harbor Healthcare, Inc., I further developed my management skills as well as a strong knowledge of health and wellness care. Through this knowledge and experience, I greatly improved the manner in which health services were provided.

By devising and applying new systems that utilized personnel and equipment more efficiently, I significantly reduced operating costs and increased time spent with patients. The end result was a more efficient organization offering higher quality healthcare services.

My education, credentials, experience, and enthusiasm for doing quality work while motivating others to do the same would be a positive addition to your organization. I look forward to the opportunity to further discuss the possibility of working for your organization. I'll call you next week to schedule a meeting; please feel free to email me.

Thank you for your time and consideration.

Best,
Elise Bentley White

Response to Job Posting on the Web

Date: Mon, 23 Apr 2000 10:40:56
From: Gonzalo L. Martinez <gonzo@aol.com>
To: job-hj50@lexmark.com
Subject: Extensive experience for Project Manager Position

My extensive experience in project management and my commitment to assembling personnel-support teams that will get the job done align extremely well with the requirements of the above job that was posted on the Career Mosaic Web site.

I am very much oriented to managing projects/schedules, and my team-building experience would be an asset to any organization looking to get the most out of its human resources while controlling costs.

I am also well versed in several software programs (MS Office, Word Perfect Suite, and SAP) and the Windows 98 and NT environments. I have set up and operated an ERP system for management of manufacturing, inventory, and sales over a wide geographical area and served on my company's automatic data-processing selection/resourcing committee.

I would like to be considered for a position in which someone of my background could make a contribution. I will contact you next week to arrange for a telephone or personal interview. Should you require any additional information, I can be contacted by replying to this email, by calling me at (256) 555-2912, or by fax at (256) 555-7740.

Best regards,
Gonzalo L. Martinez

Response to Job Posting on the Web

Demonstrates knowledge of the company. •————

Note the suggestion of a telephone interview. •————

Date: Tue, 20 Feb 2000 04:21:37
From: Matt L. Chang <changman@highnet.com>
To: Kelly Pickens kpickens@xerox.com
Subject: Ideal candidate for data analyst

Dear Ms. Pickens,

My strong commitment to a career in information technology, coupled with my database management experience and technical expertise, make me a strong candidate for a data analyst position with Xerox.

The combination of my bachelor of science degree in computer information systems and my experience in database management has enabled me to develop technical skills and allowed me to put computer training and theory into practical applications that produced solid results.

I know Xerox has an extraordinary commitment to quality, and I would like to contribute to that commitment by providing key support to the IT team.

My previous supervisors will affirm that I am efficient, hardworking, and persistent. I also have excellent time management skills, having worked full-time while attending college.

I will contact you next week to arrange for a telephone or personal interview. Should you require any additional information, I can be contacted by phone (203-555-1141) or by email.

Thank you for your time and consideration.

Warm regards,
Matt L. Chang

Response to Job Posting on the Web

Strong opening paragraph. •

She explains how her skills apply to the job she seeks. •

Date: Mon, 23 Oct 2000 01:44:03
From: Nancy Righter <nancyright@netcom.com>
To: Harry J. Fay hjfay@ariel.com
Subject: Highly knowledgeable candidate for Intermediate PC Technician

Dear Mr. Fay,

Having worked on computers for ten years and having acquired a strong knowledge of many applications from word processors to drafting programs, I am prepared for success in the intermediate PC technical position you posted on TorontoJobs.com.

My knowledge of hardware and technical procedures is a result of constant reconfiguration of my own home system as well as several years' experience developing and maintaining hospital and educational computer services. I have also acquired some formal training at the University of Toronto.

I have strong interpersonal and communication skills and enjoy working with all levels of computer users. In my job as coordinator of Patient Computer Services at Toronto Teachers Hospital, I took the opportunity to develop and maintain administrative procedures in accordance with the exacting standards of the Hospital Review Board.

Confident that my skills and experience meet your requirements, I would welcome a chance to meet with you in person to discuss your need and my suitability in greater detail. I will contact you in a week to arrange a meeting. Should you have any questions before that time, please feel free to contact me at (416) 555-6504 or by replying to this email.

Thank you for considering me.

My best,
Nancy Righter

Thank-You Letter

Johnny Ritenougher
372 Spiegel Drive
Chicago, IL 60600
(312) 555-2938

December 22, 2000

Mr. Steven Rhoads
Human Resources Director
Motorola, Inc.
1303 E. Algonquin Rd.
Schaumburg, IL 60196

Dear Mr. Rhoads,

I'd like to thank you for taking the time to discuss the recruitment officer position at Motorola with me. I very much appreciate the detail with which you described the position.

I felt a rapport with you that I know would contribute to an excellent working relationship.

You did an exceptional job of emphasizing the importance of the position to the continuing success of the company. I am convinced that I can meet the challenge of exceeding federal and state government quotas for hiring.

I also affirmed through the interview that my experience working well with students in my internship program and making positive contacts with business people in my last several jobs would contribute significantly to my success in the position. I could apply my considerable communications skills to giving presentations to graduating college seniors and selling them on working at Motorola.

I look forward to a second interview and, even more, to the possibility of contributing to both the recruitment goals and the bottom line at Motorola. As I mentioned, I am immediately available for employment.

Mr. Rhoads, thanks again for taking the time to meet with me.

Cordially,

Johnny Ritenougher

Thank-You Letter

In one of the very rare cases where a longer job-search letter is acceptable, this applicant has been recruited for an interview without ever having sent a cover letter and resume. Thus, when she follows up with her thank-you, she includes some of the detail she would have included in her cover letter.

Debbie Papadeas
343 Tobacco Drive
Winston-Salem, NC 27105
(336) 555-2132

October 11, 2000

Dr. George Lennox, Provost
University of West Carolina
Winston-Salem, NC 27105

Dear Dr. Lennox:

I want to thank you for seeking me out and taking the time to meet with me about the proposed position of Special Assistant to the Provost for Admissions Projects. I am truly excited about this position and the contribution I could make toward working with alumni, high-school teachers, volunteers, faculty, and deans on recruitment, and targeting such potential student populations as nontraditional students, international students, and perhaps others.

My strong support for the University of Western Carolina, along with exceptional communications, organizational, promotional, and marketing skills, make me exactly the kind of "value-added" employee who can get this job done for you. You need someone who can target new kinds of student constituencies, using innovative marketing skills. I am that person.

My ability to "sell" Western Carolina has many dimensions, as the College of Medicine recently learned when Dean Deepknecht contracted with me to rewrite, edit, and polish both the overall School of Medicine accreditation plan and the Nursing Department plan. As you probably know, both documents earned the highest possible ratings from the accrediting bodies, and the college plans to contract with me for the next step in the accreditation documentation process.

My work here at Western Carolina for the past several years also speaks well of my ability to promote the university. I currently handle publicity and promotion for the Favis Museum of Art. I also oversee the administration of the art department. I interact regularly with art majors, potential students, and the ten work-study students I supervise.

Finally, Dr. Lennox, I'm enclosing some ideas I've had for promoting Western Carolina and boosting enrollment. I note well your cautions that "everyone thinks they're an admissions expert." I don't pretend to be one, but I do want you to know that my mind is working on the challenges at hand.

Thank you again for your consideration of me. I look forward to the possibility of working with you.

Sincerely,

Debbie Papadeas

Thank-You Letter

Demonstrates understanding of the job requirements. •

Builds on rapport established at the interview. •

Craig B. Adelson
101 Epiphany Avenue
East Greenwich, RI 02818
(401) 555-9695

December 29, 2000

Dr. Peter Neuman
Greenwich Chiropractors, Inc.
200 E. Main Street
East Greenwich, RI 02818

Dear Dr. Neuman:

It was wonderful having the opportunity to speak with you concerning the nursing position with your practice. I know how limited a physician's time can be, and your timely involvement in the interview process impressed me. After speaking with you, I felt certain that we can develop an effective working relationship.

After reflecting on our discussion, I deduced that you are looking for more than a competent head nurse; you seek someone who can keep the entire operation in focus. Technical nursing skills are critical, and I can execute mine readily. I intend to use not only my integrity and loyalty in this position, but my open communication and managerial skills to their fullest extent.

The scope of responsibility for this position is broad and parallels my position in the United States Army. I dedicated many additional hours to becoming proficient in numerous areas, and my tenacity was quickly recognized. I would like to share the same experience with you by contributing to the success of your organization.

If you decide that I should interview with any of your partners, I will be available at your convenience. Until then, I look forward to the possibility of working with you.

Sincerely yours,

Craig B. Adelson

Thank-You Letter

Relates her understanding of the job requirements • ————
to her past experience.

Expresses willingness for a second interview. • ————

Monique Anne Bleuel
128 Watergate Blvd., #34
Washington, D.C. 20010
(202) 555-1224

August 5, 2000

Dr. Jane Billings
Washington Hope Hospital
100 C Street NW
Washington, D.C. 20009

Dear Dr. Billings,

I'd like to thank you for talking with me about the COO/Medical Data Processing Director position within your hospital. I also wish to take this opportunity to reiterate my interest in working for you at Washington Hope. I appreciate your comments concerning my qualifications and experience, and I feel very comfortable with the prospect of working with you.

After further studying the job description, I conclude that the ideal candidate should possess solid organizational and interpersonal skills, acute attention to detail, and a willingness to manage in a hands-on manner. The person selected for this position will also have to be a quick study to manage in a completely new environment and to ensure a smooth transition. I am convinced that I am a person whose skills and abilities align well with your needs.

This position is extremely similar to my position with Washington Qwik-Care, where I became proficient in management of the entire operation. In addition, my academic record attests to my dedication and penchant for learning.

I am available to interview with the IT Director and the Controller for Washington Hope.

Again, Dr. Billings, thank you for your time and consideration.

Cordially,

Monique Anne Bleuel

Thank-You Letter

Karen Handelson
2780 Ben Franklin Drive, #29
Philadelphia, PA 19500
(215) 555-7495

October 27, 2000

Mr. John Easterbrook
Vice President of Information Technology
Campbell Soup Company
Campbell Place
Camden, NJ 08103-1799

Dear Mr. Easterbrook:

Thank you for taking the time to discuss the Web Designer position with me. After meeting with you and observing the IT operations, I am further convinced that my background and future goals coincide very well with your needs.

I really appreciate that you took so much time to acquaint me with the company. That care shown to a potential employee speaks well of your management style. It is no wonder the Campbell Soup Company retains its employees for so long. I know I could learn a great deal from you and would certainly enjoy working with you.

In addition to my qualifications and experience, I will bring excellent work habits and judgment to this position. With the countless demands on your time, I am sure that you require people who can be trusted to get the job done with minimal supervision. Given my range of experience and capacity to learn, I can readily undertake the additional workload that should result from the reorganization of the accounting department.

I look forward, Mr. Easterbrook, to hearing from you concerning your hiring decision. Again, thank you for your time and consideration.

Sincerely,

Karen Handelson

Thank-You Letter

Note the warm, cordial tone. •

Patricia Stevens Longo
43 123rd Street
Bellerose, NY 11426
516-555-8652

November 1, 2000

Ms. Roberta Gregory
AT&T Corp.
32 Avenue of the Americas
New York, NY 10013-2412

Dear Ms. Gregory,

I'd like to thank you for taking the time to talk with me Monday about the corporate adjuster position you have open at AT&T.

Your energetic presentation was enough to brighten anyone's Monday morning. I really appreciate that you took so much time to acquaint me with the company and its benefits.

I also enjoyed the challenging, thoughtful talk I had with Mr. Wilson. I felt a rapport and respect for him that I know would facilitate a good working relationship.

I feel I have a good understanding of the requirements of the position, and I am very interested. I am even more confident than before of my ability to make a real contribution to AT&T.

Ms. Gregory, thanks again for talking with me Monday. Should you or Mr. Wilson want to talk with me further, I would be more than happy to oblige. I look forward to the possibility of working with you.

Cordially,

Patricia Stevens Longo

Thank-You Letter

Makes use of highlighting to recap his fit with the job. •

Note that he includes a writing sample. •

Carl Carlsburg
253 North 57th Avenue
Omaha, NE 68132
(402) 555-2029

December 4, 2000

Dr. Joel E. Newall
Director, University Relations
University of Nebraska–Omaha
Omaha, NE 68132

Dear Dr. Newall,

I'd like to thank you for taking the time to interview me for the staff writer position you have open. I enjoyed meeting with you and am confident we could have an excellent working relationship.

Especially after meeting with you, I am positive that my background and expertise are a perfect fit for the job and its requirements.

Recapping my strengths and "fit" with the position:

- My previous short-term stints as staff writer with two suburban Lincoln colleges provided excellent experience.
- My newspaper editing background would be an enormous asset because I have the inside track on what editors are looking for.
- My excellent "people skills" would enable me to fit into your congenial atmosphere as well as work well with the media and the university community.

I am also enclosing a piece I wrote expressing some of my ideas on how PR people can have greater success getting their publicity placed in the media.

Thank you again, Dr. Newall, for your time and consideration. I look forward to hearing from you around the first of the year.

Sincerely yours,

Carl Carlsburg

Key Career and Job Web Sites

While most experts stress that you should spend no more than 20 to 25 percent of your job-hunting efforts online (unless you are in a technical field), nevertheless there are plenty of great career-related Web sites that can help you with cover letters, resumes, interviewing, salary negotiation—and list job postings. Here are our suggestions for where to spend your time online. While Web sites come and go—and we can't guarantee all these Web sites will still exist throughout the life span of this book—you can always go to our site, Quintessential Careers, for the most current and complete list of career and job Web sites.

General Career Web Sites

- Quintessential Careers: A career and job-hunting resources portal, where you can find all the resources mentioned in this book—and much, much more. Special sections organized by job-seeker, industry, and geographic location. A growing library of career articles and tutorials. A free, biweekly career newsletter, QuintZine, emailed to you upon request. If you visit only one career Web site, make it this one. URL: http://www.quintcareers.com/
- JobHuntersBible.com: the official Web site and designed as a supplement to Richard Bolles' classic and enduring job-hunting book, *What Color Is Your Parachute?* (Annual, Ten Speed Press). Includes a guide to job-hunting on the Internet as well as a collection of career-related articles and other original resources. URL: http://www.jobhuntersbible.com/
- The Riley Guide: Employment Opportunities and Job Resources on the Internet— "The grandmother of resources for job seekers," and still a premier Web site, with plenty of original advice and resources, as well as plenty of links. URL: http://www.dbm.com/jobguide/

General Job Web Sites

- Quintessential Careers—The 10 Best Job Web Sites. URL: http://www.quintcareers.com/top_10_sites.html

- Career.com: Search for jobs, attend a "cyber" job fair, or post your resume—all for free. URL: http://www.career.com/
- FlipDog.com: Search for jobs (several hundred thousand are listed) or post your resume—all for free. URL: http://www.flipdog.com/
- Headhunter.net: Search for jobs (several hundred thousand are listed) or post your resume—all for free. URL: http://www.Headhunter.net/
- Monster.com: Search for jobs (several hundred thousand are listed) or post your resume—all for free. URL: http://www.monster.com/

Cover Letter Web Sites .

- Quintessential Careers—Cover Letter Resources: Find all sorts of resources and links to excellent cover-letter information, including a cover-letter tutorial. URL: http://www.quintcareers.com/covres.html
- JobStar—Cover Letters: Includes information about cover letter basics, a sample cover letter, and books and online cover letter resources. URL: http://www.jobsmart.org/tools/resume/cletters.htm

Resume Web Sites .

- Quintessential Careers—Resume Resources: A great starting point for finding all sorts of resources and links relating to resumes, including resume tutorials. URL: http://www.quintcareers.com/resres.html
- The Damn Good Resume: A great resource from resume guru Yana Parker. Information about her books, newsletter, software, and more. URL: http://www.damngood.com/

Interviewing Web Sites .

- Quintessential Careers—Interviewing Resources: Find all the best interviewing resources and links, including typical interview questions, types of job interviews, and more. URL: http://www.quintcareers.com/intvres.html
- ARCHEUS: Guide to WWW Interview Resources: From Gary Will, offers some

fantastic interview-related articles and resources. URL:
http://members.nbci.com/worksearch/intres.htm

Networking Web Sites

- Quintessential Careers—The Art of Networking: Sponsored by Katharine Hansen's excellent networking book, *A Foot in the Door* (2000, Ten Speed Press), this site has all the best networking resources (including lists of professional and trade organizations), both on and off the Web, and includes an informational interviewing tutorial. URL: http://www.quintcareers.com/networking.html
- Industry Insite: Enables you to find people online to network with who share common bonds with you: same career field, same high school, same college, same current or former employers, and more. URL: http://www.industryinsite.com/

Salary Negotiation Web Sites

- Quintessential Careers—Salary Negotiation: A great starting point for finding useful resources and links related to salaries, including a link to a salary negotiation tutorial. URL: http://www.quintcareers.com/salary_negotiation.html
- Salary.com: A nifty site for help in determining the value of a job offer or what you are worth on the job market. This site provides a vast collection of salary reports on virtually every occupation. Free. URL: http://www.salary.com/
- Jack Chapman's Salary Negotiations: An excellent resource from the author of one of the best books on salary negotiation, *Negotiating Your Salary: How to Make $1,000 a Minute* (2000, Ten Speed Press). Take the salary negotiation quiz and see if you know enough about negotiating. URL: http://members.aol.com/payraises/

Internet Access Resources

Fee-based Access and Email Services:
- AOL. URL: http://www.aol.com/
- EarthLink. URL: http://www.earthlink.net/

- MSN Internet. URL: http/www.msn.com/
- Prodigy. URL: http://www.prodigy.com/
- AT&T WorldNet. URL: http://www.att.net/
- CompuServe. URL: http://www.compuserve.com/

Free Access (and Free Email):
- Juno Online Services. URL: http://www.juno.com/
- Freeinternet.com. URL: http://www.freei.net/
- FreeLane powered by Excite. URL: http://freelane.excite.com/freelane/
- Freewwweb. URL: http://freewwwebusa.com/
- Lycos Free Internet Access. URL: http://free.lycos.com/

Free Email Services:
- MSN Hotmail. URL: http://www.hotmail.com/
- Net@ddress. URL: http://www.netaddress.com/
- Postmark.net. URL: http://www.postmark.net/
- Yahoo! Mail. URL: http://mail.yahoo.com/

Recommended Reading

Obviously, cover letters make up a small—albeit important—part of the job-search process. Here are some books that can fill in the gaps if you're unfamiliar with how to mount a major job search.

General Career Books

Career Change: Everything You Need to Know to Meet New Challenges and Take Control of Your Career, by David P. Helfand (1999, VGM Career Horizons). Voted one of the Top Ten Career Books for 1999. A great tool for job-seekers who need extra help when switching from one career to another. The real-life experiences of 10 career changers are profiled, with a special emphasis on helping disadvantaged job-seekers.

CareerXRoads 2001, by Gerry Crispin and Mark Mehler (Annual, JIST Works). This annual edition attempts to find and review only the best job, resume, and career management sites on the Web, and is a great tool for job-seekers looking for detailed reviews of all the best career and job Web sites.

What Color Is Your Parachute?, by Richard Nelson Bolles (Annual, Ten Speed Press). This enduring job-hunting bible continues to be a favorite, serving as a guiding light for those in pursuit of satisfying and fulfilling employment. This book is not a detailed guide to resumes, cover letters, interviewing techniques, and so on. It's a more basic volume directed at those who aren't quite sure what they want to be when they grow up, and those who've decided they want a new career.

Who's Hiring Who: How to Find That Job Fast, by Richard Lathrop (1989, Ten Speed Press). Something of a companion piece to *Parachute*. Bolles even calls it "the second best job-hunting guide on the market." Like Bolles, Lathrop emphasizes the hidden job market. Once you've read Bolles and know what you want to do, Lathrop will take you one step further, applying sharp marketing principles to resumes, cover letters, and interviews. Good information about interviewing, using contacts wisely, and getting maximum salary offers.

Resume Books

The Damn Good Resume Guide: A Crash Course in Resume Writing, by Yana Parker (1996, Ten Speed Press). This no-nonsense guide to resumes from the resume guru is extremely easy to follow, and it has many tips on creating effective resumes. It presents many samples of resumes and its companion volume *The Resume Catalog: 200 Damn Good Examples* (1996, Ten Speed Press) has even more.

Electronic Resumes & Online Networking: How to Use the Internet to Do a Better Job Search, Including a Complete, Up-To-Date Resource Guide, by Rebecca Smith (1999, Career Press). This book shows job-seekers how to create content-driven Web resumes, and make the Internet their most effective resume-networking tool.

100 Best Resumes for Today's Hottest Jobs, by Ray Potter (1998, MacMillan). For every type of job-seeker—college graduates, vocational/professional school graduates, women, and others—plus tips on electronic resumes and online job hunting.

The Overnight Resume, by Donald Asher (1999, Ten Speed Press). Contains the absolute latest on Internet job search, e-resumes, scannable resumes, and HTML styles. Asher covers the resume-writing process step by step and includes additional advice on the job search. He includes plenty of resume samples in a wide variety of styles and formats. Another resume book by Asher, *From College to Career: Entry-Level Resumes for Any Major* (1999, WetFeet.com), targets new graduates.

Resume Magic: Trade Secrets of a Professional Resume Writer, by Susan Britton Whitcomb (1998, JIST Works). Filled with before-and-after resume examples that not only teach the author's special techniques but also show why they work, this book divulges the secrets of better resume writing from an expert with more than a decade of experience producing powerful, effective resumes.

Networking Books .

A Foot in the Door: Networking Your Way into the Hidden Job Market, by Katharine Hansen (2000, Ten Speed Press). A highly touted book by the co-author of this book, it gives you all the tools and shows you all the techniques for successful networking and informational interviewing—keys to successful job-hunting.

Interviewing Books .

Killer Interviews, by Frederick W. and Barbara B. Ball (1996, McGraw-Hill). Based upon one author's successful work coaching thousands of job-seekers and career changers, this guide reveals the essential steps applicants must take to persuasively sell themselves in the interview process.

Sweaty Palms: The Neglected Art of Being Interviewed, by Anthony Medley (1992, Ten Speed Press). This book became the standard for the field because it talks about the real problems faced in many job interviews and what job-seekers can do to prepare for them.

Salary Negotiation Books

Negotiating Your Salary: How to Make $1,000 a Minute, by Jack Chapman (1996, Ten Speed Press). Simply one of the best books on salary negotiation in print. This book is a practical step-by-step manual for getting your best salary.

Perks and Parachutes: Negotiating Your Best Possible Employment Deal, from Salary and Bonus to Benefits and Protection, by John J. Tarrant with Paul Fargis (1997, Times Books). This helpful handbook on ways to negotiate the best employment contract offers tips on how to secure deals that include job guarantees, stock options, profit sharing, and other lucrative benefits.

Career Books for College Students

The Backdoor Guide to Short-Term Job Adventures: Internships, Extraordinary Experiences, Seasonal Jobs, Volunteering, Work Abroad, by Michael Landes (2000, Ten Speed Press). A well-written and well-designed book that is an invaluable resource for discovering adventurous and meaningful internships and short-termjobs.

College Grad Job Hunter: Insider Techniques and Tactics for Finding a Top-Paying Entry Level Job, by Brian D. Krueger (1998, Adams). A powerful job-hunting guide for college students and recent college graduates, offering great advice on all aspects of job hunting.

Dynamic Cover Letters for New Graduates, by Katharine Hansen (1998, Ten Speed Press). All the great cover letter tips and techniques, here geared specifically to college students. For example, it describes the top ten ways that college students in particular can write effective cover letters.

Major in Success: Make College Easier, Fire Up Your Dreams, and Get a Very Cool Job, by Patrick Combs (2000, Ten Speed Press). An easy-to-read book—inspirational, practical, and full of resources for the college student and recent graduate.

Index

About the Authors

Katharine Hansen is a former speechwriter and college instructor who currently provides content for the Web site, Quintessential Careers, edits QuintZine, an electronic newsletter for job-seekers, and prepares job-search correspondence as chief writer for Quintessential Resumes and Cover Letters. She is author of *Dynamic Cover Letters for New Graduates* and *A Foot in the Door: Networking Your Way into the Hidden Job Market,* as well as co-author of *Write Your Way to a Higher GPA.* She can be reached at kathy@quintcareers.com.

Katharine Hansen

Randall S. Hansen, Ph.D.

Randall S. Hansen, Ph.D. is currently Webmaster of Quintessential Careers, as well as publisher of its electronic newsletter, QuintZine. He writes a biweekly career advice column under the name "The Career Doctor." He is also a tenured, associate professor of marketing in the School of Business Administration at Stetson University in DeLand, Florida. A well-published career expert, Dr. Hansen has been writing for various academic journals, trade magazines, and Web sites for the past ten years. And he has been an employer and consultant with hiring and firing decisions for the past fifteen years. Dr. Hansen is co-author of *Write Your Way to a Higher GPA.* He can be reached at randall@quintcareers.com

With their two children, Mary and John, the Hansens live in DeLand, Florida where along with helping job-seekers succeed in their job and career goals, they enjoy gardening and riding their bikes.